Flavour

with

Benefits

France

Flavour with Benefits

France

CATHY CONNALLY
CHARLEY BEST

collesano
PUBLISHING
121 Richmond Street West, Suite 1000, Toronto, ON M5H 2K1 Canada

Contents

8   INTRODUCTION

10   PLANNING THE JOURNEY

13   A TOAST TO THE WIDOWS OF CHAMPAGNE

38   METZ AND THE MIRACLE OF AN ARTICHOKE

61   COURAGE, SACRIFICE & LOVE - VOSGES AND BURGUNDY

89   LYON - THE CAPITAL OF FRENCH CUISINE

117   MEANDERING THROUGH PROVENCE

153   MARSEILLE - MIRROR ON THE MEDITERRANEAN

187   IT'S TIME TO LEAVE

194   FLAVOUR WITH BENEFITS: SICILY & CALABRIA PREVIEW

198   RESOURCES AND TOOLS

200 RECIPE INDEX & PROFILES

204 ALTERNATIVE INGREDIENTS RECIPES

216 TOOLS FOR YOUR KITCHEN

218 STOCKING YOUR PANTRY

222 THE SCIENCE BEHIND
     FLAVOUR WITH BENEFITS

232 INDEX

236 SELECTED BIBLIOGRAPHY

236 ACKNOWLEDGEMENTS

238 AUTHORS' BIOS

Introduction

Would you love to escape on a romantic journey? Your ticket is between the covers of *Flavour with Benefits: France*.

Bienvenue! Welcome to a road trip through France featuring vignettes, or short stories about the stops along the way. Each chapter seeks to capture the beauty of the chosen places, share accounts of memorable people and introduce some inspired foods.

Would you like to go to France? If so, you're not alone. France is the world's number one travel destination – ahead of Spain, the USA, China and Italy. And if you're wondering where to go in France, any direction will delight.

The route we travel is a personal one: a mix of childhood memories, stories of women and places and flavours we love. Accompany us on a scenic road trip through parts of France you may never have seen or thought of before. In the Champagne region, learn about the women who built the champagne industry, then on to Metz, where magnificent architecture becomes the backdrop for food as medicine. Travelling southeast, we find the Vosges and Haut-Rhin villages where my grandfather fought – and nearly starved – during World War I.

Drive with us through the back roads and rolling hills of Burgundy, then visit France's culinary capital, the city of Lyon, where enterprising women took cuisine to the next level.

The next leg of our journey is magical Provence, the region where famous artists found inspiration – and where the quality of light will mesmerize you. Finally, we arrive at France's second-largest city, Marseille, with its own distinctive landscape and traditions. For details on the complete trip with all locations, see the next section, Planning the Journey.

Before taking this trip, we read everything we could to understand more about the memorable women who altered history each in their own way. Women such as Barbe-Nicole Clicquot of Veuve Clicquot Champagne House, my grandmother Stella who helped others survive the Great Depression, Eugénie Brazier of Lyon culinary fame and Julia Child who documented details of French cooking for an American audience. We found it inspiring to learn more about how they dealt with the struggles of their day and how they survived and thrived.

This is not a book on traditional French cooking and certainly not a standard cookbook. It combines some new takes on traditional favourites for health reasons, many of which are plant-based. In each chapter, there is some inspiration from the region, but the variety and freshness of the produce at French markets gave us license to take what was available and develop some non-traditional options.

Flavours are linked indelibly to some of our best memories. Culture and tradition heavily influence our food preferences, some of which are set even before we are born.

Flavour is a combination of taste, aroma and texture, but we also "eat with our eyes". All our senses are involved in the enjoyment of food and flavour. It can be fundamental to happiness and satisfaction. If someone suggests that our favourite flavours and foods may be changing, fear can strike. It is fundamental and emotional.

Understanding this, we decided to take a fresh look at some of our favourite flavours. We could not think of a more iconic place to have this conversation than France. It's the home of many famous dishes that are enjoyed around the world, even by those who have never visited the country.

We approach this topic of flavours and benefits in this way: when you invest your money, you expect to get a positive return. The same should go for your health. What you eat should be carefully considered to achieve positive health returns. This became important to us as we looked at our own food choices and the impacts they were having on our health. We thought we were eating a good diet, but the numbers at the doctor's office did not support this conclusion.

It's even more alarming when you investigate what the average diet in North America is and then look at the top seven causes of death. These include heart disease, cancer, stroke and diabetes. These are diet related. They are preventable and there is good news: we can take action without pills. Hmm. Food as medicine. Even something as simple as changing what you eat for breakfast has a positive impact; see Small Changes, Big Benefits: A Nutrition Interlude (page 66).

We were guided by scientific research in our selection of recipe ingredients and even cooking methods. This is discussed in The Science Behind Flavour with Benefits (page 222) which is dedicated to the discussion of food and its relationship to health.

There is a Recipe Index & Profiles chapter (page 200), which includes an overview of over 50 recipes, highlighting time and difficulty and designating whether the recipe is vegetarian, vegan, zero cholesterol, oil-free, a high fibre source, gluten-free, tree-nut free or enhances sexual vitality.

Where we have replaced traditional ingredients with healthier alternatives, there are the Alternative Ingredients Recipes (page 204). These include flax "eggs" (page 210) which stand in for eggs, as well as sauces such as "Cheese" Sauce (page 206) or "Worcestershire" Sauce (page 214). Many of these alternative ingredients are referenced in the recipes. In Stocking your Pantry (page 218), staples for your kitchen are listed, including ingredients that may be unfamiliar to some, such as monk fruit, which is frequently used in place of sugar. There is more discussion of monk fruit in The Science Behind Flavour with Benefits (page 228).

Please check with your doctor and other medical professionals to ensure that any dietary changes you want to make are right for you and do not impact any medications or other treatments.

Flavour with Benefits: France was completed during uncertain times. So a pleasant distraction is in order for all of us. The book is written to feel like you are chatting with a good friend at a café table, maybe even in France. We hope that you'll be inspired and make plans to visit those places that are new to you or revisit those that revive your favourite memories.

We co-wrote this book, but ultimately, we chose to make it the voice of Cathy as this book is about her journey and family history.

We took all the photographs except for those drawn from books, archives (where noted and credited) or old family photos. The food photographs were taken during our trip to France or in our kitchen at home.

Along the way, you may see some recipes that you would like to try. If you do, we'd love to hear what you think. You can leave comments at https://flavourwithbenefits.com.

And if you have the time, we would appreciate it if you would leave a book review on Amazon or Goodreads and tell us what you think.

Through these shifting times, we trust that you, and those you love, can find the strength and compassion in your lives to be happy and thrive.

Cathy Connally and *Charley Best*

"Aux saveurs! À la santé!" (To flavours! – to health!)

Learn more at: www.flavourwithbenefits.com, for Cathy on Instagram: @flavourwithbenefits and Facebook: flavourwithbenefits
for Charley on Instagram @authorofyourowndestiny Facebook: authorofyourowndestiny
Twitter: @CharleyBest6

Planning
THE JOURNEY

Planning a trip may be almost as much fun as the journey itself. It is like visiting an old friend, with treasured memories and looking forward to new adventures. Every region of France is magical. It is always fascinating and will have unexpected twists and turns. The country is so rich in the things we love – interesting people, delicious food, unique places and intriguing history.

Speaking of history, when we began researching some bits of French history, our interest was in women and their impact on modern-day cuisine and wine. While the history of French men is well documented, not as much is written about the women.

Seeking to uncover their stories helped form the itinerary: a trip to learn more about intrepid women, revisit my introduction to food as medicine in eastern France and photograph the places where my grandfather fought in World War I.

PACKING TO GO

I have decided to stay in some apartments with kitchens and also some quaint hotels. This means bringing along some favourite kitchen tools to cook and bake with local ingredients. I've also made reservations at some of the famous restaurants and champagne houses founded by women who are giants of food and wine in France.

OUR ITINERARY:

Fly to Paris, which is always a treat, and from there take a delightfully circuitous road-trip, highlighted on the next page. Along the way I'll take pictures and experience:

A Toast to the Widows of Champagne – Every tour should start with a glass of champagne and a slice of cheesecake. But did you know about the enterprising widows who built the industry?
Metz and The Miracle of an Artichoke – In the Lorraine region in eastern France, a five-year-old girl is cured by an artichoke prescribed by her doctor, instead of pills.
Courage, Sacrifice and Love – A drive through the Vosges hills and the winelands of Burgundy – reminiscing about grandparents and how small changes can lead to big benefits.
Trailblazing Mothers of Lyon – Women provided the foundation for French gastronomy. Walk through picturesque Lyon and experience the flavours.
Meandering through Provence – Inspiration in Arles and the Camargue, a dreamy artistic area which will have you wanting to eat your passport and everything else in sight.
Marseille and the Coastal Mountains, the Calanques – A time to reflect on more than the Mediterranean.

Oh, they're calling my flight. Allons-y! Let's go!

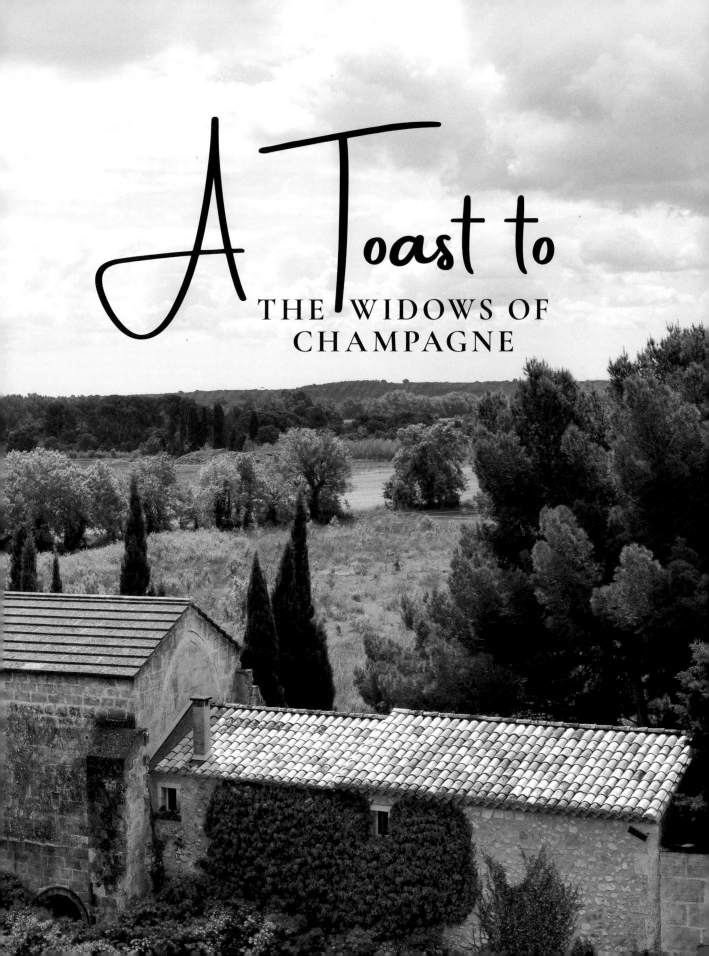

A Toast to
THE WIDOWS OF CHAMPAGNE

A Toast to the Widows of Champagne

It's Time to Celebrate!

Mansion on Avenue de Champagne - Épernay

WOMEN LEADERS AND THE CHAMPAGNE INDUSTRY

> *"I drink it when I'm happy and when I'm sad. Sometimes I drink it when I'm alone. When I have company, I consider it obligatory. I trifle with it if I'm not hungry and drink it when I am. Otherwise, I never touch it — unless I'm thirsty."*
>
> ———————
>
> Madame Lily Bollinger's retort to "When do you drink champagne?" posed by a journalist from the London Daily Mail on 17 October 1961

I like champagne. It's a reminder to have a little fun along the way. To enjoy both special occasions and the wonder of an average day. Just imagine. The pop of the cork. The spray of bubbles. The clink of crystal glasses. The toast to the moment. Can you already taste it? Feel the bubbles? Me too.

When you think of famous champagnes, who do you think of? Taittinger, Bollinger, Dom Pérignon, Veuve Clicquot, Roederer, James Bond (wait, how did he get in this conversation?) and more.

Did you know that a large number of these famous champagne "houses" became industry powers because of their women leaders? Many of them were widows, or *veuves*, and ran the champagne houses when their husbands had died. Here are a few:

The Grande Dame of Champagne – Madame Clicquot, née Ponsardin, Widow Clicquot or Veuve Clicquot (1777 – 1866) – invented blended rosé methods by naturally colouring the wine with the red grape skins, and she was an expert at blending grapes to create the finest flavours.

Louise Pommery (1819 – 1890) was credited with the creation of "brut" champagne. This allowed her to open up the English market and make the company immensely profitable, with annual sales of one million bottles. She was one of the first company directors in France to create retirement and health funds for her employees, and she even founded an orphanage in Reims.

After her husband's death, Lily Bollinger (1899 – 1977) became head of Bollinger from 1941 until 1971. She put the Bollinger House on the international stage through various marketing and bottling innovations. She offered variations of champagne that were previously unknown to consumers. She also had a warrant to supply champagne to Queen Elizabeth in 1955, and she was known to have a sense of humour, as the opening quote in this chapter demonstrates.

There are many others, including Mathilde-Émilie Laurent-Perrier and Apolline Henriot who played critical roles in the building of the champagne industry, as well.

Pretty village of Hautvillers, France

Grapes on the vine near Bouzy, France

I CANNOT VOTE, BUT I CAN RUN A BUSINESS
"YOUR HIGHNESS, WOULD YOU LIKE SOME OF MY CHAMPAGNE?"

Women. We all face challenges. When I set up and ran my first business, it wasn't easy. I'd wake up sweating in the middle of the night wondering how we were going to make payroll that month.

200 years ago, the widows of Champagne were granted more freedom to run their businesses and open bank accounts than married women or single women. "Les veuves" were marketing and selling their products during wars when they could not vote. But the Tsars, the German Royal family, and the Royals in England all demanded champagne from the houses run by the widows.

The women of Champagne rose above the social structure to achieve something exceptional – success in a time when the odds were stacked against them.

Women!

No wonder their wines sparkle and bubble. Ha. Take a bow, ladies. À votre santé! (To your health.)

I wish I could have met you all, but at least I can sip your champagnes! Now we must pay a visit to the cellars of Veuve Clicquot.

Visiting with Bernard Tornay of Bernard Tornay Champagnes, and a bottle of Coteaux Champenois Bouzy Rouge

Veuve Clicquot

"The world is in perpetual motion, and we must invent the things of tomorrow. One must go before others, be determined and exacting, and let your intelligence direct your life. Act with audacity."

Advice in a letter from Madame Clicquot to her great-granddaughter about life and business

The Champagne region is situated 160 kilometres (100 miles) northeast of Paris or about 90 minutes by car. In the beautiful city of Reims, and neighbouring Épernay, are the head offices of many of the best known champagne houses.

I'm visiting Veuve Clicquot, and specifically, the company cellars in Reims, to learn more about Madame Clicquot and one of the world's most famous champagnes.

One of the typical challenges in this journey through France was learning more about the women who had a significant impact on industries and traditions that we celebrate. The truth is, this history is underrepresented everywhere – not just in France.

The Widow Clicquot: The Story of a Champagne Empire and the Woman Who Ruled It, a New York Times #1 bestseller by Tilar J. Mazzeo, provides thoughtful research and insight into the woman who would ultimately be known as the Veuve Clicquot or Widow Clicquot. What intrigued me about Mazzeo's description of this great woman, was the confidence she showed despite the difficult conditions in her life and her struggle to make the outcome of each day better than the one before. It reminds me of many women I've known.

Barbe-Nicole Ponsardin was born into a wealthy family in Reims in 1777. At 21, she married François Clicquot, the son in a family running multiple businesses, including a small wine company led by François himself. Her husband died suddenly when she was 27. With the business struggling, Barbe-Nicole lobbied her father-in-law to take François' place and run the wine company. He agreed upon the condition that she become an apprentice winemaker and learn the technical aspects of the business. What a great challenge and opportunity! I agree with Mazzeo: the father-in-law must have been a shrewd and caring man. This one decision in 1805 meant that the new widow would become one of the first women in France to run a major commercial enterprise.

Over the years and through many setbacks, she took the technical learning to heart and pushed to remove the sediment that clouded a typical bottle of champagne. The process is known as "riddling" or *remuage* in French. Through a painstaking process initiated by Barbe-Nicole, and perfected by one of her employees, the sediment and dead yeast are removed from the second stage of fermentation, yielding a clear, crisp and sweet champagne.

During this time, Europe was at war. But with Napoleon Bonaparte's abdication in 1814, the Tsar of Russia, Alexander I, was in the mood to celebrate. Madame Clicquot and her team quietly organised a ship to store 10,000 bottles of her 1811 champagne in Amsterdam, on the bet that the war would be over soon. She was able to sell champagne to the royal court in St. Petersburg and caught competitors unaware. The 1811 vintage found great favour with the Tsar, who is said to have remarked that he would only drink "a bottle of the Widow". In my experience as an entrepreneur, these comments are good for business. Her business boomed. The courts of Europe insisted on this essential form of libation. Champagne and cash flowed. Madame Clicquot faced many other business and social

Champagne tasting room in the Veuve Clicquot caves

challenges, but she left a legacy that demanded "only the finest" – a practice that is still in place today.

The stairs she must have walked down into the company cellars are spectacular. I descend 30 metres (98 feet) into another world via a colourfully lit staircase.

> *My version of "Stairway to Heaven"*
>
> ---
>
> Veuve Clicquot Cellars

Did you know that around 80 BC, the Romans mined salt and chalk under today's city of Reims? Much later, local winemakers found that storing champagne in these caves helped it mature by providing cooler temperatures and protection from sunlight and vibrations.

According to our tour guide, the company has an inventory of 40 million bottles in the caves underneath Reims! I wonder if people deliberately try to get lost?

The distinctive colour of the Veuve Clicquot packaging was trademarked in the 1800s. It is Pantone 137c – a type of yellow. Each step in the staircase lists a year in which champagne was produced. It is not every year. The taste and quality must be perfect, echoing the Widow Clicquot's pursuit of excellence.

At this point in the tour, I realise why this champagne is famous. We taste several vintages deep in these caves. The reason that the traditional method of making champagne is so good is that it produces a fresh, crisp, fruity taste, with small bubbles that seem to last forever.

The company sponsors a prestigious business award, known as the Veuve Clicquot Bold Woman Award. It is an annual tribute to the dynamism of Madame Clicquot and honours women around the world who have built, taken on or developed a business. Her spirit and high standards live on.

> **CHAMPAGNE TRIVIA FOR YOUR NEXT PARTY:**
>
> · The Pol Roger Champagne House created *cuvée Sir Winston Churchill*, in honour of the man who drank their champagne at 11 am every day.
>
> · Marilyn Monroe once took a bath in a tub filled with 350 bottles of champagne.

Stairway leaving the
Veuve Clicquot cellars

Patio outside the Veuve Clicquot Headquarters where customers can sip champagne, Reims, France

Reims City Hall (Hôtel de Ville), the one example left of Baroque architecture in Reims after World War II

Building façade in central Épernay, France

Recipes + Flavours Inspired

BY THE CHAMPAGNE REGION

This region inspires festive parties and decorative foods. Recipes in this section pay tribute to the Widows of Champagne and iconic companies in Reims, such as Fossier Maison du Biscuit Rose. Fresh produce, a crucial element of French country life, is front and centre, as well as alternatives to traditional favourites.

STRAWBERRY RHUBARB CHAMPAGNE CHEESECAKE

A tribute to the *Veuves*, without whom we would not be enjoying this lovely drink today. This cheesecake uses – you guessed it – champagne as an ingredient. It can be decorated in several ways, either with an architectural look using Fossier Biscuit Rose de Reims to decorate the sides or with seasonal fruits taking centre stage. When you serve this one, be sure to give a toast to the ladies who started it all over 200 years ago. This cake does not use a water bath, but you might need one after eating a slice! It is easy to make and a great party dessert. Don't worry if cracks develop. The top can be decorated with fruit to hide them.

Yield: 1 cheesecake, 8 servings
Total Time: 1 hour 30 minutes + 2–4 hours chilling time
Equipment: 9" (23 cm) nonstick springform pan, parchment paper, food processor, chopsticks

FLAVOURS: The decadence of almond, champagne, sweet strawberries and tart rhubarb – all swirled to perfection.

BENEFITS: Easy to make and great for parties. Using yoghurt in place of cream cheese reduces saturated fat and calories. Using monk fruit (instead of sugar) lowers total carbohydrates and calories.

CRUST

10 Biscuit Rose de Reims, crushed or 1 cup (96 g) almond flour

⅓ cup (70 g) softened coconut oil or 4 tbsp (57 g) butter

STRAWBERRY RHUBARB MIXTURE

1½ cups (150 g) rhubarb, diced

¾ cup (150 g) strawberries, sliced

½ cup (100 ml) champagne

CHEESECAKE FILLING

3⅓ cups (500 g) Skyr 4% yoghurt (or Greek yoghurt)

2 cups + 1¾ tbsp (500 g) regular or light cream cheese

3 eggs

¾ tsp monk fruit or ½ cup (100 g) sugar

1 tbsp (13 g) vanilla extract

CRUST

Preheat oven to 350°F (177°C).

Crush the biscuits (if using) until they look much like the consistency of a graham cracker crust. I used a nut grinder to crush them finely. You could also put them into a sealable plastic bag and crush them by hand.

Place parchment paper into the bottom of the pan for easy release of the cake when finished. Cut to fit the bottom of the pan or you can purchase pre-cut parchment paper rounds.

Mix the crushed cookies (or almond flour) with the butter or coconut oil and press the mixture into the bottom of the pan with your hands until smooth. Tip: if it is too sticky, use a piece of plastic wrap to cover the mixture in the bottom of the pan and press it gently until smooth. Remove the plastic wrap.

Bake for 15 minutes or until lightly golden brown and slightly pulling away from the sides. Leave to cool.

STRAWBERRY RHUBARB MIXTURE

Place the rhubarb and strawberries into the food processor and pulse for 30–45 seconds to break them up. Do not purée.

Place contents into a medium-sized saucepan and add the champagne.

Cook for 15–20 minutes over medium heat, stirring occasionally and taking care that it does not boil over as the fizz from the champagne will froth a bit. It should reduce and thicken a little.

When the mixture is smooth, set aside to cool. Note: if you are not a rhubarb fan, you can use all strawberries in place of the rhubarb.

CHEESECAKE FILLING

Oven should already be preheated to 350°F (177°C).

In a blender or food processor, mix the yoghurt and cream cheese until smooth and creamy. Add eggs and pulse until integrated into the mixture. Add the vanilla and monk fruit (or sugar) and mix on high for 45 seconds.
Make sure all ingredients are fully incorporated. Note: Adjust sweetness to taste by adding more monk fruit (or sugar) as desired.

Pour the cheesecake filling into pan with baked crust. Smooth the top with a spatula.

Pour half of the strawberry rhubarb mixture on top of the cheesecake filling and use chopsticks or wooden skewers to stir the mixture gently into the cheesecake giving it a swirl effect. Do not overmix.

Make sure not to touch the bottom of the pan while stirring in the rhubarb mixture. You do not want to mix the crust into the cake.

Bake for 30 minutes uncovered and then up to an additional 10 minutes with foil on top to prevent too much browning. When the cheesecake is baked, it will move a little in the centre but will have a *done* look. The edges of the cake should pull away from the sides of the pan slightly. Do not overbake as it will dry out.

Let the cake cool on the counter until it reaches room temperature. This will reduce cracking. Cover with foil or plastic wrap and transfer to the refrigerator for 2–4 hours or overnight. Any cracks will be covered by the rhubarb mixture and decorations.

Remove from the refrigerator and let the cake warm up for 5–10 minutes. If it has not pulled away from the sides of the pan, carefully insert a dull wet knife around the inner edge of the pan. Gently release the spring and remove from the pan. You can decorate the top with the remaining half of the rhubarb mixture. Other serving suggestions are rhubarb ribbons, fresh fruit or crushed Biscuit Rose de Reims scattered on top.

NUTRITION: *(per serving)*
1 slice, monk fruit | sugar

Calories	363	410
Fat	31.1 g
Saturated Fat	18 g
Cholesterol	147 mg
Carbohydrate	11.9 g	24.4 g
Fibre	1.1 g
Protein	10.7 g
Sugar	1.5 g	14 g
Sodium	298 mg

Imperial Porcelain 1744, St. Petersburg, Russia with a tribute to *Biscuit Rose de Reims*

TRIBUTE TO BISCUIT ROSE DE REIMS

Before arriving in France, I dreamt of these pink biscuits from Maison Fossier. They're impossible to find in North America, but when I was shopping in Arles, I found them right there on the shelf. Barely able to contain my excitement, I bought several boxes, but I wanted to bake them myself. The recipe, which dates back to 1690, is a closely guarded secret. Through help from friends and trial and error, this recipe emerged. They originated as twice-baked bread dough, or *bis-cuit,* which means cooked twice in ancient French. The biscuits were flavoured with crushed vanilla seeds, which were black. To mask the black colour, some red colouring was added, resulting in these pretty biscuits. Ammonium bicarbonate (a predecessor of baking powder) was used to leaven the biscuit dough. Pastry with a history.

FLAVOURS: Vanilla with sweetness and a hint of yeast, and when you dip them in a cup of coffee – heaven.

BENEFITS: Pure fun with a bit of history as you take a bite and enjoy them.

Yield: 10 pink biscuits
Total Time: 50 minutes
Equipment: Baking forms, piping bag, cookie sheet, silicone mat, wooden skewers (or toothpicks)

1 large egg, separated

1 tsp clear vanilla extract

4 tbsp (50 g) sugar

¼ to ½ tsp red food colouring

⅜ cup (45 g) all-purpose flour

2¾ tbsp (21 g) cornstarch

½ tsp instant yeast

¼ cup (25 g) icing sugar

Preheat oven to 350°F (177°C).

Whisk egg yolk, vanilla extract and sugar until white and fluffy.

Add egg white and the red food colouring (a bit at a time) and mix to get the colour desired. Use a wooden skewer to dip into the dye and then stir into the mixture. Whisk for 2 minutes. Note: Use a new skewer every time you dip in the dye to prevent contamination.

Whisk the dry ingredients: flour, cornstarch and yeast in a small bowl. Add the dry ingredients to the wet ingredients with a spatula and mix thoroughly to form a batter.

Place a silicone mat onto a large, flat cookie sheet. Oil the baking forms.

Put the batter into the piping bag and cut a small hole in the bottom of the bag.

Pipe the mixture evenly into the bottom of the forms. It should spread out after piping the batter. It will also smooth out a bit as it bakes.

Sprinkle with icing sugar and allow it to rest for 20 minutes to form a crust.

Bake for 15–20 minutes. Let them cool. Use a dull knife to carefully remove the biscuits from the forms. Dust with more icing sugar as desired.

.

NUTRITION: *(per serving)* 1 biscuit	
Calories	64
Fat	0.6 g
Saturated Fat	0.2 g
Cholesterol	19 mg
Carbohydrate	13.6 g
Fibre	0.2 g
Protein	1.2 g
Sugar	8 g
Sodium	7 mg

CRUNCHY KALE, FENNEL & CABBAGE SALAD

To balance the decadence of cheesecake and biscuits, this lively salad will fill the air with the welcoming aromas of fennel, basil and lemon. It's fast and easy to make, and you can change the ingredients based on what you have on hand, with no sacrifice on taste. Most of these ingredients are readily available all year.

FLAVOURS: The strong aromas and flavours of fennel and fresh basil are contrasted with the sweetness of carrots, the earthiness of onions and a tart splash of lemon juice.

BENEFITS: With a big contribution to your daily fibre intake, this little beauty is low-calorie, cholesterol-free and loaded with folate, potassium, calcium and vitamin K. Feel full longer without that sluggish feeling.

Yield: 6 servings
Total Time: 20 minutes
Equipment: Sharp knife, mixing bowl

2 cups (200 g) red cabbage, diced

2 cups (150 g) red or black kale, finely diced (or baby kale leaves)

1 medium stalk (100 g) fennel, diced with ends trimmed

5–6 fennel fronds, chopped

¾ cup (100 g) onions, diced

4 small tomatoes (275–300 g), diced

⅓ cup (100 g) cauliflower, diced

⅔ cup (100 g) carrots, diced

10–12 (30 g) fresh basil leaves, rolled and sliced

⅓ cup (84 g) balsamic vinegar or lemon juice

½ tsp sea salt or tamari

½ tsp black pepper, ground

1 tsp smoked paprika

8 basil leaves for garnish

pink peppercorns for garnish

Mix diced and sliced vegetables in a large salad bowl.

For those who are wary of kale, chop it very finely, like confetti. Mature kale can sometimes be tough in bigger pieces, so this is an important step. You can even include the stalks, which are high in nutrients too.

Mix vinegar (or lemon juice) and hot sauce in a small bowl and pour over salad. Mix until well distributed.

Sprinkle salt, pepper and smoked paprika on the salad and mix well.

Decorate individual salads with large basil leaves and pink peppercorns. Other options to consider for toppings include walnuts or, for added heat, hot sauce. Use your imagination to spice it up.

NUTRITION: *(per serving)*
6.7 oz (190 g)

Calories	56
Fat	0.4 g
Saturated Fat	0.1 g
Cholesterol	0 mg
Carbohydrate	11.2 g
Fibre	3.6 g
Protein	2.8 g
Sugar	4.6 g
Sodium	208 mg

CULTURED CASHEW "CHEESE"

It would not be France if we did not have cheese on the menu. For those of us who love cheese, and there are many of us, now there is an easy way to make your own cheese. It is plant-based and delicious. You can flavour it any way you want. It can be served with fruit and crackers or even on top of a pizza. In just a few short days, you will have cultured "cheese". Use cashews or almonds as the base. It has a lovely tangy taste.

FLAVOURS: That cheesy taste you crave spiced up with herbs such as smoked paprika and tarragon.

BENEFITS: Zero cholesterol, lower in saturated fats than regular cheese and easier on the calorie count.

Yield: ¾ cup "cheese"
Total Time: 2½ days
Equipment: Food processor, glass bowls with plastic covers, cheesecloth, wooden or plastic spoon

2 cups (300 g) raw cashews or blanched slivered almonds

2–4 garlic cloves, pressed

2 tbsp (60 ml) lemon juice

½ tsp tamari or soy sauce

2–6 tbsp nutritional yeast

½ cup (118 g) rejuvelac* water or regular water

2 probiotic capsules**

Add smoked paprika, seeds and dried herbs to decorate

NUTRITION: *(per serving)*
5 tbsp (75 g)

Calories	167
Fat	12.8 g
Saturated Fat	2.5 g
Cholesterol	0 mg
Carbohydrate	10.2 g
Fibre	1.3 g
Protein	5.2 g
Sugar	1.5 g
Sodium	107 mg

Place cashews in a medium bowl of cool water. Soak for 6 hours. Almonds do not require soaking. Drain cashews thoroughly and place them into the food processor. For almonds, place into food processor unsoaked and use the highest setting to maximize texture.

Add garlic, lemon juice, nutritional yeast and tamari, and process until smooth. Add the rejuvelac (or water) a little at a time until the consistency is creamy. Scrape down the sides of the food processor as needed.

Taste the mixture and see if you want to add more nutritional yeast, garlic, tamari or lemon juice.

Transfer the mixture to a glass bowl. Open the probiotic capsules and empty contents into the bowl and using a wooden or plastic spoon, mix thoroughly into the "cheese" mixture.

Scoop the "cheese" mixture and place it onto two layers of cheesecloth. Wrap it tightly and secure with a rubber band. Put the "cheese" onto a paper towel and into a bowl.

Leave it out on the counter for 48 hours. Taste to see if the right amount of tanginess has developed. If not, let it ferment on the countertop for up to 72 hours.

Place into a tightly covered container and put it into the refrigerator for 6 hours.

For a fancy presentation, take a section of the "cheese" and roll it into a log. Next, roll the log onto smoked paprika, herbs and seeds. Cut into slices and serve with crackers, fruit, etc.

Best served chilled. It can be used to top pizza too, but it will not melt. It will keep for a week or more in the refrigerator.

* Rejuvelac is fermented water from sprouting grains. It is used as liquid in making cultured cashew "cheese".

**These can be found in health food stores or at a pharmacy.

Thank you to Kristen Wood/moonandspoonandyum.com for recipe inspiration.

CAROB APRICOT WHOLE WHEAT SOURDOUGH BREAD

The practice of making sourdough bread or naturally leavened bread has thousands of years of history. For me, bread baking is therapy. Feeling the dough become cohesive and then stretching and folding the bread, building the gluten – it's magical. The thrill of the first look at the "bloom" of the bread as it bakes and the familiar aroma is intoxicating. There is a reason many people practice this ancient tradition. And then there are also the health benefits of fermented foods.

This recipe was inspired by King Arthur Baking Company's Pain au Levain. For more on sourdough starters and baking, refer to *Sourdough: Recipes for Rustic Fermented Breads, Sweets, Savories and More* by Sarah Owens.

You will need sourdough starter to make this bread. I use rye starter because it is vibrant and flavourful. White flour starter can also be used, but try to use organic flour as the fermentation process of a naturally leavened starter intensifies the ingredients. It's best to avoid any chemicals or pesticides in the flour and your bread.

Yield: 2 loaves, 20 servings
Total Time: 20–32 hours
Equipment: Large mixing bowls, measuring spoons, 2 shower caps (or plastic wrap), 1 baker's scale, 2 brotform (proofing) baskets, French oven or pizza stone, parchment paper, bread thermometer, lame, pizza peel

FLAVOURS: The beautiful tang of sourdough with a pungent blend of nuttiness and sweetness from the added carob, dates and apricots.

BENEFITS: Fermented foods improve digestion and mineral absorption. Whole grain rye and whole wheat flours have complex carbohydrates with added nutrition. Dates and apricots add sweetness without sugar. Carob adds calcium and is an antioxidant.

LEVAIN

1¼ cups (149 g) organic unbleached all-purpose flour

⅓ cup (74 ml) room temperature water, 70°F (21°C)

2 tbsp (28 g) ripe (fed) sourdough starter – white flour or rye flour

DOUGH

all of the levain

2 cups + 2 tbsp (482 ml) water, 75°F to 80°F (24°C to 27°C)

5 cups (600 g) organic whole wheat flour

¾ cup (81 g) dark rye flour, organic preferred

1 cup (160 g) dried apricots, diced small

¼ cup (25 g) carob powder

scant ½ cup (56 g) dates, diced small

¾ tbsp (13–17 g) sea salt

Making naturally leavened bread is not difficult, but it does require some dedication and planning. Since there are long fermentation times, it is best to determine what time to start making the levain and bread so you do not end up with middle-of-the-night tasks. I generally check my starter and feed it a few hours before I start my levain. This means that the best time to feed the starter in order to have it ripe for this recipe is around 4 pm. That way, in a few hours, you can make the levain.

To make the levain, knead together all the levain ingredients in a large bowl until they form a smooth, stiff dough. Use plastic wrap or a clean shower cap to loosely cover it for 12 hours. It will need to ferment at room temperature. It's best to do this overnight. For rye starter, you will know it's ready when you pull on it and there are obvious gluten strings. If using white flour starter, it should have doubled in size and be domed at the top or just beginning to sink in the middle.

To make the dough, break up the levain into small pieces with a dough scraper or bench knife. It will be sticky. Add it to the dough water. Wait 5 minutes to let it absorb the water. This will make the dough easier to manage. Add the remaining ingredients (except the salt) until all the flour is fully absorbed. Make sure to evenly distribute the fruit and carob powder. If using a stand mixer, mix on the lowest speed for 2 minutes with the dough hook attachment.

Cover the bowl with the shower cap and let it rest for 30 minutes.

Knead the dough for 3 minutes by hand or 1½ minutes on speed 2. The dough will be sticky.

Allow the dough to rise in the bowl for 60 minutes, covered with the shower cap. Sprinkle the dough with a touch of water, add the salt and pinch it into the dough until it is fully incorporated.

Give the dough the first stretch and fold after 60 minutes. Do two more stretch and folds at 30-minute increments. Up to four is optimal.

Gently divide the dough in half using a baker's scale. It is best to get the dough even in weight. Put the two loaves on a well-floured surface and shape them into rounds and leave them to relax for 20 minutes.

Flour your brotform baskets thoroughly and place each loaf top side down into each basket. Make sure the dough is not separated on the bottom. Use your hands to "stitch" the bottom of the dough together if it is separated.

Cover the baskets with shower caps and leave on the counter for 2 hours. Alternatively, place the covered baskets in the refrigerator for up to 16 hours.

Preheat the oven to 450°F (232°C). Place covered empty French oven or pizza stone in the cold oven and allow to heat up for about 45 minutes.

Remove the shower caps from the baskets. Place a piece of parchment paper on a pizza peel or on a small lightweight cutting board. Place the parchment paper-covered peel or cutting board on top of the basket and carefully flip or invert the loaf and carefully lift the basket off the dough. It should come off easily if properly seasoned. If not, let gravity work and hold it until it comes loose. Score the loaf with a razor blade or lame.

Using oven mitts, open the oven door and carefully remove the lid of the French oven and place to one side. Carefully pick up dough in parchment paper, holding it on each side, and lift it into the French oven. You can manoeuvre the dough slightly in the pan, if needed. Alternatively, you can use the pizza peel to jiggle and slide the dough in the parchment paper into the French oven. You want it to be centred evenly in the pan. Once the dough is in the French oven, put the lid back on and bake for 30 minutes. Do not open the oven during the first 30 minutes.

After 30 minutes, take the lid off the French oven and set aside on the stove or hot pad. Bake the bread uncovered for 15 minutes more. Remove from oven and take the bread out to cool. Bake the second loaf with the same instructions but allow the pan to reheat for 15 minutes. Cool the bread completely before slicing. It will stay fresh for 1–2 weeks.

Alternatively, you can bake both loaves at the same time on a pizza stone with parchment paper on top. Preheat the pizza stone just as you did with the French oven. Place a pan, with one cup of hot water, in the bottom rack of the oven to create steam. This keeps the bread from drying out. Be sure to use oven mitts and keep your face back to prevent a steam burn when you open the oven. Bake the bread for 35–40 minutes. The bread should have a hollow sound when tapped. It should have an internal temperature of 195–200°F (90°C–93°C). Put the finished loaves on a wire rack to cool completely before slicing. They will stay fresh for 1–2 weeks.

NUTRITION: *(per serving)*
1 slice, 1½ oz (40 g)

Calories	140
Fat	0.7 g
Saturated Fat	0 g
Cholesterol	0 mg
Carbohydrate	29.4 g
Fibre	5.1 g
Protein	5 g
Sugar	2.3 g
Sodium	211 mg

Metz

AND THE MIRACLE
OF AN ARTICHOKE

The Temple Neuf (New Temple) on Île du Petit-Saulcy surrounded by the Moselle River in central Metz

I've Come Back to Remember

Fancy dining on the cruise to France – SS United States (Mom, Cathy, Dad and Tom)

MY FIRST TRIP AWAY FROM HOME

When I was five, we moved to the city of Metz in eastern France. It was here that I had some formative experiences. I have come back to retrace that time and give thanks. (*Je suis revenue ici pour me souvenir et rendre grâce.*)

We had been living in Connecticut when my father, Aaron, was awarded a Fulbright scholarship. We moved to Metz where he would teach English and American literature at a local *lycée* – a boy's high school. He had been recommended based on his excellent French, and the appointment was highly anticipated by my parents.

I vaguely remember our family sailing on the SS United States from New York to Le Havre on the Normandy coast of France. To this day, that ship still holds the transatlantic record for the fastest east and west crossings of the Atlantic.

Anne Urquhart and Dorothy Marckwald, the two decorators who designed the interior, were determined to create a modern ambience inspired by the Art Deco style. This might be where I became a fan of this decor. The cabin-class dining room had midnight-blue walls with contemporary art.

Each night, we would dress up and have a formal dinner at tables topped with white tablecloths and fancy silver sugar bowls and creamers. For dessert, we were served *Petit Fours* (tiny decorated cakes).

Exterior of the Cathédrale Saint-Étienne de Metz

Life in Metz

NEW LANGUAGE, NEW SCHOOL

The city of Metz is the capital of the French region known as Lorraine. The massive Gothic Cathédrale Saint-Étienne de Metz is famed for displaying the largest expanse of stained glass in the world (6,496 square metres), including three windows by Marc Chagall. The famed Gregorian chant was created here in the 8th century. With many beautiful gardens and bridges over the Moselle and Seille rivers, the city has much to explore.

Metz Kindergarten (école maternelle)   Cathy – Top row third from the left

Fort Moselle - Kindergarten (école maternelle)

Smile! – Tom and Cathy outside the apartment

I was enrolled in an école maternelle (nursery school) at five and didn't know one word of French, but I soon became fluent. My father taught me new words every day. When I first invited a friend over and wanted her to wait for me, I ran to ask my father how to say the words in French. When I returned and said, "S'il-te-plaît, attends ici," she did exactly as I asked. I giggled and was so pleased. Since then, I've become very good at asking people to do things!

There was also a little boy in my kindergarten class who teased me unmercifully. His name was Patrick-Michel, but I called him Patrick Méchant (Wicked). Giving him the gift of my *repartee* in French was quite empowering.

I also fell in love with the French cheeses and bread I saw in the local shops. Walking with my mother, Mary, and looking up at ancient buildings and the cathedral was a far cry from being a little girl in Connecticut. Let's go on a walk and I'll show you.

First, I want you to see my school in Fort Moselle. It still looks the same. My mother would take me here every morning and pick me up at midday.

Above, you can see my brother and me in front of the apartment complex where we lived, which was just a few blocks from my school. My father taught me to ride a bike with no training wheels and just when I thought I needed him to hang on to my bike, he let go and I was riding on my own. My brother Tom and I loved riding our bikes and playing in the courtyard and at the local park.

Food as Medicine

IT ALL STARTED WITH AN ARTICHOKE

Let's visit the *Marché Couvert de Metz* (Metz covered market) just across from the main cathedral. As a little girl, I loved all the enticing foods – especially chocolate, cheese and nuts. I mean, who could resist?

But I became quite ill almost immediately after arriving in Metz. My parents noticed that my stomach had become distended and took me to a local doctor. She declared, *"C'est son foie*!" (It's her liver!)

The doctor gave my parents the solution to the problem. The artichoke. Welcome to one of the many power foods in the world. In French, it's called *artichaut*.

It helped save my liver. No wonder the French are experts in this area since they love wine, cheese and rich, fatty foods, all of which stress liver function.

At five, I started eating artichokes and also had to curtail my three favourite foods: chocolate, cheese and nuts.

Desserts galore!

Artichokes – One of many wonderful foods that can improve one's health. It helped a five-year-old, me.

Walking the aisles at the Marché Couvert de Metz (Metz covered market) near the Cathédrale de Metz in central Metz, France

Cathédrale Saint-Étienne de Metz main entryway

As I understand it, eating artichokes helps remove toxins, lowers cholesterol levels and cleanses the liver. The liver metabolises compounds that produce free radicals. Artichokes have powerful antioxidants that scavenge free radicals. The liver performs many critical functions that help filter and neutralise poisonous substances in the body.

The bloating in my stomach gradually receded, thanks to eating steamed artichokes almost every day – not taking pills. The cause of the problem was treated naturally. Now, that's Flavour with Benefits!

I'll always hold the memory of Metz close to my heart and give thanks to the French doctor and the artichoke. This miraculous vegetable is both delicious and healthy. Some of my favourite ways to eat them are included: Steamed Artichokes with Mustard Sauce (page 48) and Artichoke Hummus (page 51).

As a tribute to my time in Metz and the many food specialties in the Lorraine region, I've included my versions of Quiche Lorraine Nue (page 55), Plum and Cherry Torte (page 56), as well as some surprising alternatives for your favourite vegetable side dishes and grab-and-go snacks.

The outside market beside the Marché Couvert de Metz

Recipes + Flavours Inspired

BY METZ AND THE LORRAINE REGION

I hope you enjoy the food inspired by Metz and a few childhood memories. They include a beautiful steamed artichoke and hummus made with artichokes, which is a bit more unusual. Because artichokes were so important to my early health, I have crafted these recipes to share with you.

STEAMED ARTICHOKES WITH MUSTARD SAUCE

Preparing fresh artichokes can be daunting. With all those thorns and unfriendly looking leaves, they can be a little intimidating. They are from the thistle family, after all. But they are healthy, easy to prepare and great to eat. You can steam and dip the leaves and artichoke heart in a spicy Dijon mustard sauce.

Yield: 2 large or 6 small servings
Total Time: 35 minutes
Equipment: Large pot, steamer insert, tongs, small bowl, ramekins

2 large artichokes (about 680 g) or 6 baby artichokes

¼ cup (59 ml) apple cider or balsamic vinegar

2 tsp Dijon mustard

1 tbsp (10 g) garlic powder

2 tbsp (30 ml) filtered water

1 tsp dried parsley or thyme

1 tsp nutritional yeast

NUTRITION: *(per serving)*
1 large artichoke with mustard sauce

Calories	109
Fat	0.4 g
Saturated Fat	0.1 g
Cholesterol	0 mg
Carbohydrate	21 g
Fibre	9.7 g
Protein	6.8 g
Sugar	2.6 g
Sodium	109 mg

FLAVOURS: Fresh steamed artichokes have a lovely subtle nutty flavour which is complemented by the spicy mustard sauce. Many people discard the leaves, but they are mighty tasty and worth the work.

BENEFITS: These great-tasting vegetables are loaded with vitamins, minerals and fibre. They have been used for centuries to lower blood sugar levels and improve liver health. The sauce is high in B vitamins.

If you are using large artichokes, cut them in half with the stems on. Baby artichokes can be left whole. Trim stem ends.

Fill a large pot with 5–6 cups of water and place a steamer basket inside. Bring it to boil. The water should just reach the bottom of the steamer basket.

When the water is boiling, turn the temperature down to medium.

Place the larger artichokes in the steamer, making sure they are standing up and not covering each other. Steam for 15 minutes and then turn them over for an additional 15 minutes. For baby artichokes, steaming time may be closer to 20 minutes total. You can turn them over after 10 minutes to ensure all parts are cooked.

You can test when they are cooked by putting a fork into the bottom of the artichoke (the stem). If it is soft, the heart is done. Then, attempt to pull a leaf off of the artichoke. It should come loose easily. If not, steam some more until it releases easily.

Put the vinegar, water, mustard, garlic powder, dried herbs and nutritional yeast in a small bowl. Mix thoroughly and pour into the ramekins.

To serve, give each person 1 large artichoke (or 3 small ones) and sauce. Pull each leaf off and dip into the sauce. Use your teeth to scrape the meat off the bottom of the leaf. Discard the rest of the leaf. When you get down to the tiny immature leaves, remove them with a fork and discard. Cut the artichoke heart into pieces and dip into the sauce and eat with a fork. You can substitute mustard sauce with butter if you are not a mustard fan.

ARTICHOKE HUMMUS

I love hummus and I love artichokes, so I created artichoke hummus! This recipe uses steamed artichokes, so please refer to Steamed Artichokes with Mustard Sauce (page 48). Even though this hummus is healthier than the standard version because it doesn't use oil, it is still full of flavour. If you want it spicier, you can add hot peppers. I like it served with raw cut vegetables such as carrots, celery, sweet peppers, cauliflower and broccoli. Alternatively, you can serve it with chips or crackers.

FLAVOURS: Add the sweet nutty taste of artichokes to the smooth creamy texture of chickpeas and you have a beautiful combination with a spicy surprise of hot peppers.

BENEFITS: These great-tasting vegetables are loaded with vitamins, minerals and fibre. They have been used for centuries to lower blood sugar levels and improve liver health. The chickpeas are rich in fibre, which slows digestion and assists in weight management. The use of water instead of oil makes this a low-calorie and low-fat snack option.

Yield: 6 servings (about 750 g)
Total Time: 45 minutes
Equipment: Food processor, spatula, measuring spoons

2 large artichokes (120 g), steamed, leaves separated and artichoke hearts diced

1 large can (540 g) chickpeas, no salt added and rinsed

½ tsp dried sriracha pepper

3 tbsp (45 g) almond butter or tahini

½ tsp salt or to taste

½ tsp pepper

¼ cup to ⅓ cup (60–80 ml) water

carrot confetti & slices to decorate

chia seeds or baked chickpeas to decorate

Remove the larger artichoke leaves from the artichoke and use a spoon to scrape the meat off the lower part of the leaf. Put the meat into a food processor. Discard the leaves.

Scrape off and discard the furry inner leaves until you get to the artichoke heart.

Cut the artichoke hearts into pieces and add to the food processor.

Put the remaining ingredients in the food processor (except water) and process on a high setting for 2–3 minutes or until smooth. Add water a few tablespoons at a time until desired consistency is achieved.

Garnish with carrot confetti and chia seeds.

Serve with cut raw vegetables such as carrots, celery and sweet peppers.

NUTRITION: *(per serving)*
4½ oz (125 g)

Calories	222
Fat	6.9 g
Saturated Fat	0.6 g
Cholesterol	0 mg
Carbohydrate	31.9 g
Fibre	10.6 g
Protein	11.5 g
Sugar	5.2 g
Sodium	255 mg

STEAMED ASPARAGUS WITH "HOLLANDAISE" SAUCE

Try a favourite brunch sauce, but with a healthier twist. Using white beans instead of dairy, gives the sauce texture, while nutritional yeast gives a cheesy taste complemented by the earthiness of the asparagus. What's more, the sauce keeps for a while when chilled.

FLAVOURS: A creamy texture with a nutty cheesy taste makes this sauce incredibly versatile.

BENEFITS: This is low in fat and high in fibre, and loaded with B vitamins and minerals, making it a winner on taste and nutrition.

Yield: 12+ servings (2½ cups) sauce, 4 servings asparagus
Total Time: 15 minutes
Equipment: Blender, saucepan, wooden spoon, pot with steamer insert and tongs

SAUCE

½ cup (125 ml) water

1¾ cups (250 g) canned navy beans (or cannellini beans)

2 tbsp (30 ml) apple cider vinegar

2 tbsp (30 g) tahini

¼ cup (18 g) nutritional yeast

½ tsp turmeric powder

1 tbsp (16 g) Dijon mustard

¾ tbsp (20 g) arrowroot starch

1 tsp garlic powder

1 tsp onion powder

½ tsp Himalayan black salt

⅛ tsp cayenne powder

ASPARAGUS

2 cups (250 g) asparagus spears

SAUCE

Put all of the ingredients into the food processor or blender and blend for 30–60 seconds or until smooth.

Pour the ingredients into a small saucepan over medium-low heat. Heat for 5–10 minutes, stirring occasionally, and serve over vegetables such as potatoes, asparagus or portobello mushrooms.

Note: Do not substitute the Himalayan black salt with regular salt or the sauce will not have the egg taste. The sulphur content in black salt has an egg flavour.

ASPARAGUS

Trim the ends of the asparagus spears. Steam the asparagus in the steamer pan for 5–8 minutes. The asparagus should turn bright green. Remove and serve immediately.

NUTRITION: *(per serving)*
3 tbsp sauce (42 g) and ½ cup asparagus (63 g)

Calories	86
Fat	2.2 g
Saturated Fat	0.3 g
Cholesterol	0 mg
Carbohydrate	12.3 g
Fibre	5.5 g
Protein	6.1 g
Sugar	1.6 g
Sodium	42 mg

QUICHE LORRAINE NUE (NAKED QUICHE LORRAINE)

Traditional Quiche Lorraine has a crust, but, believe me, naked is always better. Drop the crust and enjoy this one any time! Have seconds. These are made in a cupcake pan which makes them easier to serve than the traditional version in a pie pan. This version is gluten-free too.

FLAVOURS: The balance of tartness and saltiness wakes up your taste buds; and with the crunch of the leeks and aromatic herbs, and saltiness of the cheese, this dish offers a sophisticated blend of flavours.

BENEFITS: Lower in calories, and high in fibre and protein, it is loaded with vitamins A, C and K which are key for wound healing and bone health.

Yield: 9–10 mini quiches
Total Time: 1 hour
Equipment: Cast-iron skillet, large spoon, spatula, small mixing bowl, cupcake pan (preferably metal), sharp knife

1-2 tbsp (15–30ml) filtered water

1 cup (90 g) leeks, diced

1 small purple (or red) onion (70 g), diced

3 mushrooms, diced

½ tsp tamari

ground black pepper to taste

1 small stalk of celery, finely diced

1 small carrot peeled and diced or shredded

¼ cup (60 ml) aged vinegar, balsamic or other wine vinegar

15 cherry or grape tomatoes (255 g)

½ tsp dried thyme

½ tsp dried basil

⅓ cup (50 g) blue cheese, cubed or crumbled

2 large eggs

1¼ cups (300 ml) milk or lactose-free milk

Preheat oven to 350°F (177°C).

Grease the muffin tins with spray cooking oil. Heat the cast-iron skillet to medium-high heat and add 2 tablespoons of water. Add the leeks, onions, mushrooms, and sauté. Add tamari and cook for 3–5 minutes. Season to taste with ground pepper. Stir constantly to prevent burning.

Add celery, carrots and vinegar. Sauté for 2–3 minutes. Stir in cherry tomatoes. Cook until they are browning, then carefully pierce them with a sharp knife to release the juices. Cook for 2–3 more minutes.

Stir in thyme and basil. Spoon the contents evenly into cupcake cups.

Whisk the eggs and milk together in a small bowl. Spoon contents evenly into the cupcake cups.

Bake for 30 minutes. Let them cool slightly and carefully remove using a large spoon. Sprinkle crumbled blue cheese on each quiche and serve hot.

NUTRITION: *(per serving)*
1 mini quiche, 2¼ oz (65 g)
with Blue Cheese | without Blue Cheese

Calories	178 | 159
Fat	3.6 g | 2 g
Saturated Fat	1.6 g | 0.5 g
Cholesterol	46 mg | 41 mg
Carbohydrate	35 g | 34.9 g
Fibre	4.8 g | 4.8 g
Protein	5.8 g | 4.6 g
Sugar	22.9 g | 22.9 g
Sodium	120 mg | 43 mg

In the spirit of paying tribute to old classics, this torte is a cake version of Mirabelle Plum Tart. It is sugar-free if you use monk fruit and does not have a crust, so you can have a larger piece because it is lower in saturated fats. It's easy to make using a 9" (23 cm) or 10" (25 cm) springform pan.

FLAVOURS: This moist and tender cake is bursting with both sweet and tart flavours from the ripe plums and cherries. Adding cherries lends more colour to this simple cake.

BENEFITS: By replacing the sugar with monk fruit, this lower-calorie treat answers the need for sweets without the extra calories. Great for seconds.

Yield: 8 pieces
Total Time: 1 hour 15 minutes
Equipment: 9" (23 cm) springform pan, spatula, wooden skewer, measuring cups, mixing bowls, parchment paper

½ tsp pure monk fruit or 1½ cups (300 g) sugar

6 tbsp (85 g) unsalted butter

2 cups (240 g) all-purpose flour sifted

2 tsp baking powder

1 tsp nutmeg or mace

4 large eggs

16 small plums, halved and pitted (1.056 kg)

10–12 cherries (50–60 g) to garnish (or substitute with other seasonal fruits)

1 tsp Ceylon cinnamon

Preheat oven to 350°F (177°C).

If you are using sugar, cream the butter with the sugar. Otherwise, just cream the butter alone. Mix the monk fruit, flour, baking powder, nutmeg (or mace) in a separate bowl. Add the flour mixture to the butter mixture and stir just until blended. Add the eggs and beat until combined.

Spray the inner edge of the pan with oil, but do not spray the bottom. Put parchment paper on the bottom of the pan. Spoon the batter into the pan and place plums and cherries with cut sides up on top of the batter. Lightly press them into the batter. Sprinkle the top with cinnamon.

Bake for 45 minutes. Check the cake by piercing it with a wooden skewer to see if the batter is baked or still raw. Bake for another 10–15 minutes as needed.

Serve it plain or optionally with ice cream or whipped cream.

NUTRITION: *(per serving)*
1 slice, 6 oz (170 g)
with monk fruit | with sugar

Calories	293	433
Fat	11.7 g
Saturated Fat	6.3 g
Cholesterol	105 mg
Carbohydrate	13.6 g
Fibre	3.3 g
Protein	7.3 g
Sugar	16 g	53.5 g
Sodium	93 mg

RASPBERRY OATMEAL BARS

This healthy treat is great for those times when you need a grab-and-go snack. The raspberries will satisfy your sweet tooth, but make no mistake, these bars are fibre-rich, low in calories and cholesterol-free. They are easy to make and a good recipe for teaching children how to bake.

FLAVOURS: Raspberries provide a lovely layer of sweetness complemented by the chewy texture of oats. The bars are nicely spiced with aromatic nutmeg and cinnamon, giving them a warm and nutty taste.

BENEFITS: This snack is low in calories and high in complex carbohydrates, making it a great alternative to traditional sweets. The raspberries are rich in antioxidants which prevent inflammation.

Yield: 9 bars
Total Time: 45 minutes
Equipment: Whisk, mixing bowls, measuring cups and spoons, 9" x 9" (23 cm x 23 cm) nonstick pan, foil

1 cup (120 g) whole wheat pastry flour

1 cup (97 g) old fashioned oats (not quick oats)

½ cup (50 g) almond flour

½ cup (40 g) coconut sugar

½ tsp ground nutmeg or mace

¼ tsp sea salt

2 flax "eggs" (see note 1)

⅓ cup (75 g) almond butter

½ cup (118 ml) water

6 oz (170 g) fresh or frozen raspberries (see note 2)

Preheat oven to 325°F (163°C).

Mix all the dry ingredients together.

Add the almond butter to the flax "eggs" and mix thoroughly. It will be slightly foamy. Add the water to the almond butter flax eggs mixture and stir until fully incorporated. Add the wet ingredients to the dry ingredients and mix thoroughly until a moist dough is formed.

Take about ½ of the dough from the bowl and spread in the bottom of the nonstick pan. It will take a little work to spread it evenly.

Place the raspberries in a bowl and mash them. Spread the raspberries evenly over the dough. Tear the other half of the dough into pieces and cover the raspberries as much as possible. Smooth with a spoon slightly. The dough will spread out somewhat as it bakes.

Bake for 20 minutes lightly covered with foil. Remove the foil and bake for another 10 minutes or until golden brown. Do not overbake as they may become tough.

Cool for 10 minutes in the baking dish. Cut into 9 bars and serve.

Note 1: In a small bowl, add 2 tablespoons of ground flaxseed (preferably golden flaxseed) and mix with 6 tablespoons of warm water. Let sit for five minutes until it has a gel-like consistency.

Note 2: For frozen raspberries, defrost them slightly, gently break them apart and mash and spread over the dough.

Thank you to Driscoll's for recipe inspiration.

NUTRITION: *(per serving)*
1 bar, 2 oz (57g)

Calories	158
Fat	2.5 g
Saturated Fat	1.2 g
Cholesterol	0 mg
Carbohydrate	30.8 g
Fibre	2.9 g
Protein	3.3 g
Sugar	12.1 g
Sodium	51 mg

Grandfather Roy's mess kit from World War I etched with the names of French towns

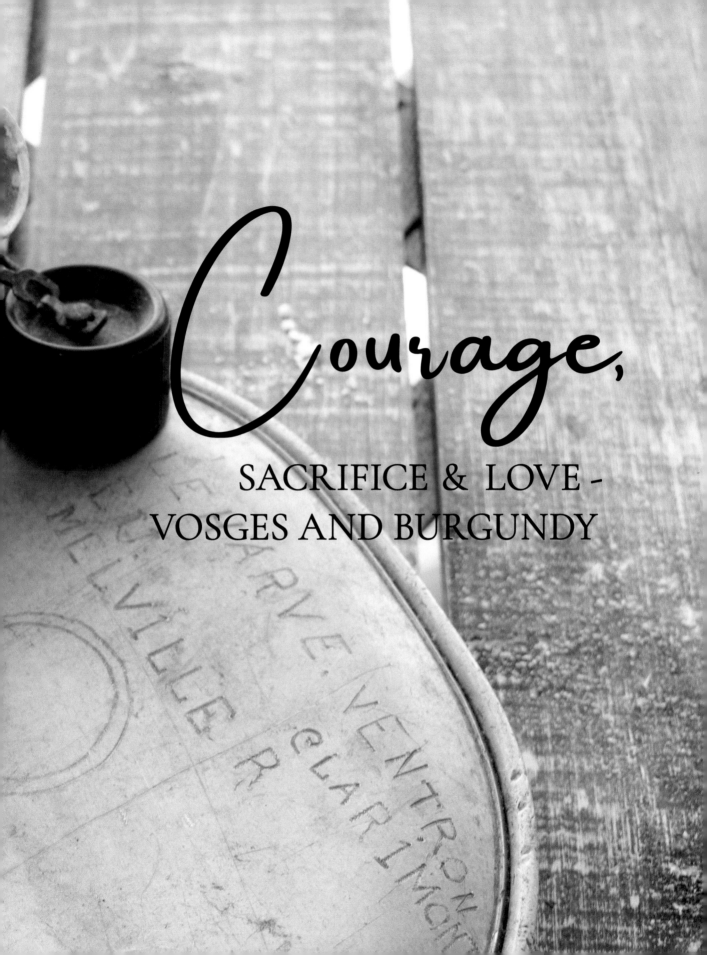

Courage,

SACRIFICE & LOVE -
VOSGES AND BURGUNDY

Thoughts of My Grandparents

DRIVING FROM METZ TO LYON

This drive is long and necessarily circuitous. In this chapter I will tell you stories about my family's connection to France, overcoming daunting challenges, and taking care of themselves and their loved ones.

The first part of my day's travel takes me through the beautiful Vosges mountains, not far from the French-German border. I stop in the villages of La Bresse, Ventron and Kruth. In La Bresse, there is a Saturday market occupying the main street. I wander through the crowd. The smells of freshly baked pastries tease me. They know I'm weak. Everything smells better in France.

A mountain valley on the road from La Bresse to Kruth in the Vosges region of France

Roy

THANK YOU, GRANDFATHER

Just over one hundred years ago, these hills were full of opposing armies and deadly conflict. Today, there is a dusting of snow on the hilltops and tall trees. A beautiful, peaceful place. I wonder if the hills can still feel the marching of troops. For me, the nearby mountains still echo with the sounds of gunfire and human anguish.

The smell of coffee wakes me from my musings. I think of a man whose name was Roy. I'm reminded of sacrifice and how fragile life is. His World War I mess kit is shown below (and on pages 60 and 61). He was my grandfather.

He was a private in the American Expeditionary Force (AEF) and fought in France in 1917 and 1918. I chose to visit these towns (La Bresse, Ventron and Kruth) because Roy carved their names into his mess kit as his unit from Kansas and Missouri moved through the area during the German occupation.

Rations, when available, were canned meat and vegetables. He once told my father that he carved the names onto the mess kit, with a knife he found, in order to take his mind off the lack of food, a common occurrence.

Grandfather, Roy Everett, in 1918

I'm thankful that he survived the horrors of war and made it home to meet and marry my grandmother, Stella.

Grandfather, thank you for being the man you were and for the impact you had on your family.

Did you know that your name, Roy, is derived from the French word *roi,* meaning "king"? I thought you should know, sir.

Grandmother Stella Everett and her children

MY GRANDMOTHER - SURVIVAL, STRENGTH...AND FOOD

Stella was born in 1902 to a loving mother, Leticia Jane. Her father, however, was an abusive man. Stella gave birth to her first child when she was seventeen years old. Roy was the only man who did not shun her for being an unwed mother.

Roy asked Stella to marry him and settle in Liberal, Kansas. They lived in a very modest house where they had three more children, including my father.

Stella loved girls. She doted on me and encouraged my fondness for pretty dresses. One memorable time, she gave me $5 to buy a bracelet to accompany the dress she had given me. When I took the money and the bracelet to the cashier to pay, the cashier *took*

the $5 from me. I sobbed and said, "I wanted the bracelet and the $5."

Not much has changed for me today. Given a dose of retail therapy, I would still like the money and the purchases.

Stella was a big woman, over 6 feet tall, strong and feisty. Her husband was a bit eccentric, an inventor and an occasional poker player. He was quite opinionated, which led to many disagreements with employers.

Stella's life was not easy. She worked many jobs, including running a local ice factory. One day, the owner told her that he was giving the other employee, a man, a raise but that she wouldn't be getting one, even though she managed the place for him. She asked him why, and he said that the man had to take care of his family, while Stella had a husband to take care of her. Not being someone to accept injustice, she quit. The owner complained, "But Stella, how will I run the place without you?" She replied, "I guess that man can do it for you." She became a parole officer and finally found her calling as a telephone switchboard operator for AT&T.

During the Great Depression, she shared eggs from her chickens and milk from her cow with neighbours and friends.

One of my favourite Stella stories is about her husband, Roy, and the weekly allowance of $1 to buy household necessities. Roy complained that Stella was spending too much. She reportedly threw the dollar at him and told him he could do the shopping. A few hours later, he returned home with very little food and told her she could do the shopping from now on.

She made a small amount of money go a long way.

Later in life, Stella developed type 2 diabetes. Her love of fried food and sweets was her undoing. The doctor gave her a strict diet to follow, which she did, but she continued to enjoy her *favourite* foods as well. Sadly, the disease progressed unmercifully.

There was no place like home, for Stella.

She missed the musical prairie winds of Kansas whenever she was away.

A summer visit to my grandmother's house in Liberal, Kansas

I DREAMT ABOUT HER

Dreams are funny, aren't they? Glimpses of light, shadows and people. In my dream, I'm an adult. I go to see her. She is surprised I'm there. I tell her I love her and that I want to make her something special to eat. So I find myself in my kitchen, but somehow in her house, and I decide to make her something tasty. I think it was two different dishes. She liked to eat a lot. I placed the food in front of her and she began eating. I started asking her things, but I can't remember what they were. What I do remember is the sound of her voice. It made me feel good. She smiled as she ate the food and said I was a good granddaughter.

I woke crying.

I wish I'd had more time to show her how food could have managed her diabetes and blood sugar levels.

I miss her energy and attitude. We all have strong women in our backgrounds who've persevered under difficult circumstances. Without them, society does not function.

Small Changes, Big Benefits:

A NUTRITION INTERLUDE

Knowing how Stella constantly struggled with her weight and health, was heart-wrenching for me, especially because it led to her early death. This example from her life combined with my own health issues, caused me to take a deeper look at the foods I was eating. Medications were not an option for me due to side effects. Reading and learning more about nutrition became a passion. After taking some online and in-person classes, I realised how much there was to know about food and how little I really knew.

But I was certain about one thing in my food choices: I would not compromise on flavour. Great flavour is what we expect and look forward to. Flavour with Benefits was born with the goal of implementing small changes in the foods we eat and over time, achieving big health benefits, while always keeping flavour at the forefront.

So, I decided to start with the beginning of each day: breakfast!

At our house, we'd been accustomed to "heartier" meals to kick off the day, sometimes accompanied by fruit. What do I mean by hearty? Sometimes, bacon and eggs with toast. Other times, bagels with cream cheese and some yoghurt. You get the idea. All very tasty.

I did some research about the nutritional value of these typical breakfasts and noted that depending on my other meals during the day, my family was off to a calorie and fat-rich start to each morning. Couple this with a hectic lifestyle of running a business, other grab and go meals and intermittent exercise routines, waistlines were growing, as were other health problems.

It was time to make a change.

By just changing my breakfast, I noticed that my body started to look different. My weight was more stable and my blood work was hitting normal levels. We all love positive feedback, so I started weighing myself each morning. I wanted to see the effects of my new breakfast regimen.

So what did I do? I combined oatmeal with two or more delicious seasonal fruits (bananas, apples, pears, blueberries, raspberries, pitted cherries, blackberries, kiwi) and a very slight sprinkling of nuts (sliced almonds, cashews, walnuts), or I ate healthy granola with maca and cinnamon. Then I would have a slice of delicious whole wheat or sourdough bread with either a modest amount of nut butter or avocado. Breakfast was transformed.

We all know that it's the little things that often make the difference. These changes were not dramatic but incremental – and they worked. Without great flavours, I'm sure we would have drifted back to older and less healthy alternatives.

The result was a 50% decrease in calories, zero cholesterol, decreased sodium/salt and sugar and a substantial increase in carbohydrates and fibre. The one change that confused me in our new breakfast regimen was protein. It decreased by more than 50%. Bad, right? No. As it turns out, we were getting too much protein throughout the day, which then turns into excess weight over time. Finally, we topped off these health improvements with more vitamins and minerals from the fruits, vegetables, and grains we were eating.

Being a dip and sauce lover, I started making Crudités with Dipping Sauce (page 73), and I couldn't stop eating those vegetables with that cool, fresh sauce. No guilt and lots of crunchy goodness. I think Stella would have loved it.

A whole world of plant-based meal options opened up. It was clear that the choices were limited only by my imagination. I realised that much-maligned vegetables, such as a potato, can become Baked French Fries (Frites au Four) (page 168) and sweet potatoes can be transformed into Sweet Potato Fries (page 81). It was never the vegetables themselves that were the problem. It was the preparation methods. The tradition of frying made them unhealthy, but with a simple change, they are back on the menu. Small changes in this area yielded big benefits in the reduction of cholesterol and saturated fats.

But let's not forget desserts. Oh no! Never sacrifice flavour or fun. The first crack at refining classic desserts meant using lower-calorie substitutions such as yoghurt instead of cream cheese or cream. Using plant-based sweetening options such as monk fruit or dates, instead of refined sugar, became standard for my desserts, including Lemon Lavender Luxury Cheesecake (page 145). Everyone enjoyed them. Maybe there was something to this.

Then I began wondering if some of these favourite desserts could be 100% plant-based and oil-free. To my surprise, many worked. Substitutes for dairy, eggs and extracted oil helped the nutrition profile, but the taste and enjoyment were still there. These include Chocolate Mousse – Avocado Surprise (page 105), Double Chocolate Fudge Brownies (page 185), Gâteau d'Arles (page 138) and even the must-have Classic Banana Bread (page 85). I was thrilled because a life without my favourite flavours did not sound inviting. Nope. Don't settle. Healthy foods do not have to be boring and tasteless.

These changes have been exciting. They have taken some time, but the results are noticeable and substantial. There were some immediate economic benefits with plant-based foods. For example, many plant-based milks have a longer shelf life, so there is no need to throw out sour milk. Loading more fruits and vegetables into the grocery cart instead of meat and cheese reduced my food budget.

But the most significant changes are that I have more energy, I have more control in my life and over my well-being. I sleep better, and I have greater sexual vitality. Feeling good and sexy is great. There is also a feeling of contentment, and this allows me to take on life's many daily challenges.

Now, let's see more of France. Stella would approve!

Several climats (plots) just outside of Nuits-Saint-Georges in the Burgundy region

I Need a Break from Driving

Vineyard off the D974 road heading south towards Beaune, Burgundy, France

Wine and cheese from Burgundy – Delicious!

One of the many fine châteaus along the Route des Grand Crus in Burgundy

As I leave behind the Vosges region and thoughts of my grandmother, I drive for several hours through beautiful countryside before reaching the famous Burgundy wine route, known as the Route des Grands Crus. Between Dijon and Santenay, the route winds for 60 kilometres (37 miles) through picturesque villages and rolling countryside.

I stop near the town of Nuits-Saint-Georges to buy some fine local wine and take pictures of the vineyards laid out with such beautiful geometric designs. The towns are typically surrounded by vineyards (thus the "village" appellation or grading), and then on the west side of the route, the vineyards begin their ascent towards forests and the beautiful hills and limestone escarpment of the Côte d'Or.

The wines on the slopes are generally given higher ratings: Grand Cru (the best) and Premier Cru (very good). The slopes allow the grapes to be drained more effectively and to obtain the greatest amount of sunlight.

I wander through the back roads of this region taking a few photographs and generally enjoying the moment. Making wine is everything here. Hundreds of years ago, the Cistercian monks in this area played an important role in winemaking and in the classification of the land (*terroir*). I'll have to come back here someday. I've heard that the cheeses are also fabulous, and I'll definitely need more time to sample them.

Now onto Lyon, the capital of French gastronomy, but first I'll leave you with foods inspired by this region and my grandmother Stella.

ROUTE DES GRAND CRUS HIGHLIGHTS:

- Côte de Nuits in the north focuses on red wine
- Côte de Beaune in the south focuses on white
- The Burgundy *climats* (wine plots) received UNESCO World Heritage status in 2015

Recipes + Flavours Inspired

BY STELLA, ROY AND THE BURGUNDY REGION

Many inspirations come to mind as I drive through Burgundy, such as Roy's near starvation as a soldier and Stella's struggle with diabetes. That's why I've included an eclectic mix of recipes. Some are meals Stella made for her family, while others are flavourful plant-based meals that everyone can enjoy.

CRUDITÉS WITH DIPPING SAUCE

This is a classic French favourite. It is flexible and can be changed to include or exclude any vegetables that are in season or to cater to your likes and dislikes. The vegetables can be consumed raw. This is healthy and faster to prepare. Alternatively, you can blanche some veggies if you think they are too hard for children or adults who have issues chewing. The white hemp seeds give the sauce a nice fresh look.

> **FLAVOURS:** Fresh veggies with the sweetness of carrots and sweet peppers, the tartness of cherry tomatoes, and the satisfying crunch of cauliflower and broccoli. But it's the spicy white dipping sauce that makes these veggies addictive.

> **BENEFITS:** Low in calories, zero cholesterol, rich in fibre and high in vitamins and minerals. No chips needed!

Yield: 1 platter of vegetables and 1¾ cup dipping sauce
Total Time: 25 minutes
Equipment: Blender or food processor, knife

WHITE DIPPING SAUCE

½ to ¾ cup (118–177 ml) water

1 cup (169 g) shelled hemp seeds

¾ tsp tamari, soy sauce or salt

2 cloves (10 g) garlic (for less spice, use 1 tsp garlic powder instead)

1 tsp onion powder

1 tsp ground mustard seed

3 tbsp (45 ml) apple cider vinegar or lemon juice

1 tsp dried dill, crushed

½ tsp cayenne pepper

½ cup (75 g) purple (or red) onion, diced

WHITE DIPPING SAUCE:

Blend all the ingredients in a blender or food processor and set aside until needed. There will be more than enough for the crudités platter presented here. Sauce can be refrigerated for 7– 10 days.

VEGETABLE PLATTER:

Cut the vegetables into bite-sized sticks so that they can be easily picked up and dipped into the sauce. Arrange the veggies around the dipping sauce bowl and serve immediately. This is incredibly nutritious and a great alternative to corn chips. Note: Nutrition facts are based on vegetables included in the picture.

VEGETABLE PLATTER
Use the vegetables you have available. Some suggestions are:

14 cherry or grape tomatoes (125 g)

2⅓ cups (150 g) cauliflower florets

1 cup (175 g) broccoli florets

4 cups (200 g) carrots

⅔ cups (100 g) small sweet peppers

Other suggestions:
Bok choy, celery, zucchini, aubergine (eggplant), larger green, red or yellow sweet peppers and hot peppers.

NUTRITION: *(per serving)*
¼ platter & 7 tbsp (117 g) dipping sauce

Calories	251
Fat	13.7 g
Saturated Fat	2.8 g
Cholesterol	0 mg
Carbohydrate	28.6 g
Fibre	5.9 g
Protein	8.1 g
Sugar	11.9 g
Sodium	324 mg

LEEK, POTATO, ONION & EDAMAME SOUP

All the greens in this soup are beautiful as well as healthy. This simple soup will most likely become one of your go-to meals. It is easy and fast, and the ingredients are readily available any time of the year.

FLAVOURS: The leeks and onions give a sweet flavour and the potatoes are rich and comforting. The blend of flavours is sophisticated and aromatic.

BENEFITS: This soup is low in calories, rich in fibre, iron, and the edamame beans have a healthy dose of calcium. A heart-healthy and filling meal with all the protein and complex carbohydrates your body needs.

Yield: 6 cups (4 servings)
Total Time: 45 minutes
Equipment: Large pot, sharp knife

Ingredients
2–4 tbsp (30-59 ml) water
⅓ cup (50 g) onions, chopped
3 large garlic cloves (15 g), pressed
1–2 tsp tamari
3¾ cups + 2 tbsp (900 ml) low-sodium organic vegetable broth
¾ cup (160–170 g) leeks, sliced in rings
½ cup (140 g) baked potato, sliced into bite-sized pieces
1⅓ cups (110 g) edamame beans (removed from pods)
2 tsp marjoram
2 tsp tarragon
1 tsp dried parsley
1 tsp dried chives
2 tsp miso bean paste

Heat a large pot and add 2 tablespoons of water and onions and sauté for 5 minutes.

Add the pressed garlic and add 1 teaspoon of tamari and the vegetable broth.

Stir and deglaze the pan. Add the rest of the ingredients and bring to a soft boil.

Turn down the heat to low and simmer for 20–30 minutes. Taste and add the additional teaspoon of tamari if needed.

Serve immediately.

Note: If sodium is a concern, eliminate the miso bean paste.

NUTRITION: *(per serving)*
1½ cups (365 g)

Calories	146
Fat	2.3 g
Saturated Fat	0.3 g
Cholesterol	0 mg
Carbohydrate	24.7 g
Fibre	4.1 g
Protein	6.5 g
Sugar	5.5 g
Sodium	365 mg

ROASTED SPATCHCOCK CHICKEN AND VEGETABLES

Given that Stella raised chickens in her own backyard, chicken dinners were undoubtedly a favourite. This spatchcock (or flattened chicken) is a tribute to Stella – and takes the humble roasted chicken up a few notches. What's unique about this recipe is that the chicken is roasted in the oven and then finished on the barbeque grill.

French cuisine's love of chicken was celebrated by the late Julia Child. While she was filming her TV show, it was done in one take. Occasionally missteps would happen and stay in the show. She encouraged her audience to just get on with it and don't be a perfectionist. What a woman! We miss you Julia.

> **FLAVOURS:** Roasted chicken basted in onions and garlic needs no introduction. Carrots glazed in maple syrup and coriander add sweetness that shimmers. The tartness of the tomatoes and the crunch of the architectural Romanesco broccoli round out the texture of the dish.

> **BENEFITS:** This meal provides high protein, offset by the fibre in the tasty vegetables. Removing the skin from the chicken reduces saturated fats. Garlic, onions and tomatoes are also heart-healthy.

Yield: 1 roast chicken serves 4, based on 7 oz (200 g) of skinless chicken per person
Total Time: 1 hour 30 minutes
Equipment: Sharp knife, large roasting pan, foil, cast-iron or frying pan, BBQ grill, large pot, steamer insert, poultry shears

4 tbsp + 2 tsp (63 ml) avocado oil (or other high temperature oil)
1 tsp sea salt
2 tsp ground black pepper
3 tbsp (18 g) fresh tarragon or 3 tsp dried tarragon
6 cloves garlic (30 g), pressed
1 medium chicken (2.25 kg), flattened, skin removed
8 medium organic carrots (488 g), peeled, greens trimmed but intact
2 tbsp (40 ml) maple syrup
1 tsp coriander powder
1 large purple (or red) onion (150 g), diced
6 Romanesco broccoli florets (100 g)
6 cherry tomatoes (224 g), red or yellow, sliced for garnish

ROAST/BBQ CHICKEN:

Preheat oven to 425°F (218°C).

In a small mixing bowl, put 4 tablespoons of avocado oil, salt, pepper and tarragon and 5 cloves of pressed garlic and mix into a paste.

Rub the garlic mixture all over the chicken. Put the chicken into a foil-lined roasting pan.

Place the chicken in the oven and roast for 30 minutes. Reserve extra chicken drippings from the pan and set aside for serving.

Remove from the oven and put the roast chicken on foil on the BBQ grill for about 10 minutes. Use a meat thermometer to check to see that it is cooked all the way through. It should register 165°F (74°C) in the thickest portion. Let the chicken rest for 10 minutes before serving.

While the chicken is cooking, prepare the vegetables.

ROASTED CARROTS:

Heat a frying pan over medium-high heat and add 1 teaspoon of oil. Swirl carrots in oil. Turn down the heat to medium and pour in the maple syrup and add the coriander. Sauté the carrots for 10–15 minutes or until tender. Cover with foil and set aside if they are ready before the chicken is done. Serve hot.

SAUTÉED GARLIC AND ONIONS:

Heat a frying pan over medium heat and add 1 teaspoon of oil, diced onions and 1 clove of pressed garlic. Sauté for 5–6 minutes until onions are translucent. Cover with foil and set aside.

BLANCHED ROMANESCO BROCCOLI

These do not take long, so prepare them right after the chicken is removed from the oven and is resting.

Take the large pot and steamer insert and lightly salt the water. Bring to a boil. Turn down to medium heat.

Place florets into the steamer tray and blanch/steam for 5 minutes. Immediately remove from the heat, put them into a bowl and place in the freezer for 5 minutes. This will retain the colour.

Remove from the freezer and use some of the extra juice from the chicken to pour over the florets when serving.

TO SERVE

Serve ¼ chicken, roasted carrots and Romanesco broccoli to each person. Pour garlic, onions and the set aside chicken drippings over the broccoli and chicken. Add cherry tomatoes as a garnish to each plate.

Note: Please use a high-temperature oil to make this dish. Do not use extra virgin olive oil, as it is not rated for high temperatures and will smoke, which is not healthy.

HOW TO FLATTEN A CHICKEN

If you cannot get the chicken cut and flattened by the butcher, rinse the chicken and pat dry. Place the chicken breast-side down on the cutting board. Using sharp poultry shears, cut along both sides of the backbone. Discard the backbone or use for soup later.

Turn the chicken breast-side up and open the underside of the chicken, much like opening a book. Use the heel of your hand and press firmly against the breastbone until it cracks. Remove wings and use for stock.

NUTRITION: *(per serving)*
¼ chicken (200 g) & vegetables

Calories	495
Fat	17.5 g
Saturated Fat	4.8 g
Cholesterol	181.3 mg
Carbohydrate	20.2 g
Fibre	4.3 g
Protein	62.1 g
Sugar	10.5 g
Sodium	508 mg

SWEET POTATO FRIES

These are baked "fries" – and they are delicious. Dispense with the idea that it takes refined sugar or maple syrup to get sweetness. Try this version of a traditional favourite and you'll be convinced.

FLAVOURS: The natural sweetness of the sweet potatoes, paired with delicious pumpkin pie spices and vanilla, make these "fries" addictive without the guilt.

BENEFITS: Satisfy your sweet tooth with sugarless sweetness and aromatic spices. Without the oil, the calories are low and there is no cholesterol. Have seconds!

Yield: 4 servings
Total Time: 35 minutes
Equipment: Sharp knife, sheet pan, parchment paper, small bowl

2 orange sweet potatoes (227 g)

2 white (or other colour) sweet potatoes (227 g)

1 tsp vanilla extract

2 tsp cinnamon

1 tsp nutmeg or mace

½ tsp ground ginger

½ tsp coriander

2 vanilla beans or cinnamon sticks, to garnish (optional)

Preheat oven to 425°F (218°C).

Wash the sweet potatoes carefully and cut out any bad pieces. Leaving the skins on, cut the sweet potatoes in half lengthwise and put the flat side down. Cut in half lengthwise again. Now cut the fries into the size you want. Try to keep them the same size to get consistent results. Thicker fries will take longer to bake.

Spread the fries in a single layer into a pan lined with parchment paper.

Bake for 15–20 minutes. They should start to slightly blister. Jiggle the fries and turn them over with tongs to get even baking. Bake another 5–10 minutes as needed.

Mix cinnamon, nutmeg, ginger and coriander in a small bowl. Drizzle vanilla extract over the fries and sprinkle the cinnamon mixture over each serving of fries. Put vanilla extract into a dipping bowl and serve hot. Add vanilla beans or cinnamon sticks for decoration in dipping bowl.

NUTRITION: *(per serving)*
3½ oz (100 g)

Calories	119
Fat	0.3 g
Saturated Fat	0.2 g
Cholesterol	0 mg
Carbohydrate	27.6 g
Fibre	4.7 g
Protein	2.1 g
Sugar	5.7 g
Sodium	72 mg

DAD AND STELLA'S CORNBREAD WITH A SURPRISE

It was a challenge feeding a large family during the Great Depression. This cornbread pays tribute to those hard times but also includes some updates that add unexpected flavours. One staple was cornbread, and a rare treat was fresh peaches. Why not marry these together? And with our love of France and iconic foods, we must add some aged French blue cheese.

FLAVOURS: This divine cornbread is both salty and sweet. The moistness of the peaches is a surprising addition and makes this recipe unique.

BENEFITS: This one is pure comfort food. The peaches provide natural sugars, fibre and vitamin C.

Yield: 1 loaf, 8 servings
Total Time: 35 minutes
Equipment: Mixing bowls, sharp knife, cast-iron skillet 9-10" (22-25 cm), wooden skewer, pie server

Ingredients
1 cup (143 g) yellow organic cornmeal
¼ cup (30 g) organic unbleached all-purpose flour
¼ tsp sea salt (pinch)
¼ tsp baking soda
1 large egg, slightly beaten
1 cup (175 g) fresh peaches, diced
1 cup (250 g) full-fat plain yoghurt
½ cup (118 ml) full-fat milk
¼ cup (50 ml) canola or avocado oil
1 tbsp (15 ml) honey
¼ peach (56 g), cut into thin slices but not separated

Preheat oven to 400°F (204°C). Lightly spray oil into the skillet and wipe out excess. Set aside.

Combine the dry ingredients, in one bowl and whisk together well.

In a second bowl, combine and stir the wet ingredients including diced peaches, until well incorporated.

Add the dry ingredients into the wet ingredients and mix until well moistened. Do not overmix, as this will cause the cornbread to break and have odd peaks.

Pour the batter into the cast-iron skillet. The batter should level itself out without help.

Fan out the sliced peach and place it into the middle of the pan. Do not press it down. The peach will drop a little during the bake.

Bake for 20–23 minutes. Check at 20 minutes. A wooden skewer should come out clean when inserted into the middle near the peach. The cornbread should be brown and the edges crispy.

Let it cool for 5 minutes. Cut pieces with a pie server right in the pan. Serve with more peaches and French blue cheese.

NUTRITION: *(per serving)*
1 slice, 3½ oz (100 g)

Calories	156
Fat	4.2 g
Saturated Fat	0.8 g
Cholesterol	25 mg
Carbohydrate	26.2 g
Fibre	2.1 g
Protein	4.5 g
Sugar	6.6 g
Sodium	117 mg

CLASSIC BANANA BREAD

This recipe originated with my mother, Mary, who typed it out for me, and I made it so many times, the paper became stained with droplets of ingredients. The original version was loaded with refined sugar and butter. This adaptation is vegan and also free of oil and sugar. If you love banana bread, this one will surprise you because it's full of flavour while delivering health benefits that the traditional version cannot. Mom's advice: use bananas that are really old and the skins are almost black.

FLAVOURS: Aged bananas have had time to develop the natural sugars and aromatic flavours that make this a great family favourite. The sliced banana topping provides moistness normally supplied by the oil.

BENEFITS: Low in calories and saturated fats with zero cholesterol, this bread can be enjoyed anytime. Substituting flaxseed for eggs increases heart-healthy omega-3s and provides a good dose of potassium. Using monk fruit means no added sugar and adds sweetness without the downsides.

Yield: 1 loaf, 10 servings
Total Time: 1 hour 30 minutes
Equipment: Loaf pan 8" x 4" (20 cm x 10 cm), mixing bowls, sharp knife, whisk, parchment paper, wooden skewer

2 flax "eggs" (see note)

½ tsp monk fruit or ½ cup (100 g) sugar

3 tbsp (45 g) almond butter

2 tbsp (30 ml) filtered water

1 tsp vanilla extract

2 tbsp (31 g) nondairy yoghurt

1 tbsp (15 ml) apple cider vinegar

3–4 medium-sized aged bananas (350 g), mashed

2 cups (276 g) whole wheat flour

1 tsp baking soda

16–20 pistachios, crushed or ¼ cup other nuts

1 banana (118 g), cut in half lengthwise

Preheat oven to 350°F (177°C). Or if you are using a dark pan for baking, set the temperature to 325°F (163°C).

In a medium bowl, blend monk fruit (or sugar) with flax "eggs". Add almond butter, 2 tablespoons of water and vanilla extract and mix until fully incorporated. Set aside.

Mix vinegar and nondairy yoghurt in a small bowl. After it curdles slightly, stir a few times, then add to the wet ingredients. Add the mashed bananas and mix well.

In a medium bowl, whisk the flour and baking soda together. Add to the wet ingredients and stir until thoroughly combined. Do not overmix. Fold in pistachios or other nuts.

Line the pan with parchment paper, even if you are using a nonstick or ceramic pan. It should help the bread release easily.

Pour the batter into the loaf pan. Push the batter slightly higher at the edges than at the centre. Place the banana halves in the middle. A nice look is to place them with the curves facing outwards. They will move apart as it bakes.

Bake for 1 hour and check doneness with a wooden skewer inserted in the centre. Bake up to an additional 20 minutes, checking at 10-minute intervals. A foil cover can be used after 1 hour to prevent over-browning. Do not overbake.

Remove from oven and let cool for 1 hour before removing from pan and serving.

Note: Add 2 tablespoons of ground flax seed (preferably golden flax seed) and mix with 6 tablespoons of warm water. Let sit for five minutes, until it has a gel-like consistency.

NUTRITION: *(per serving)*
1 slice, 3 oz (85 g)
with monk fruit | with sugar

Calories	178 | 216
Fat	4.1 g
Saturated Fat	0.5 g
Cholesterol	0 mg
Carbohydrate	31.6 g | 41.6 g
Fibre	2.9 g
Protein	4.6 g
Sugar	6.3 g | 16.3 g
Sodium	110 mg

CHOCOLATE DONUTS WITH CHOCOLATE FROSTING

Many of us crave fatty indulgences like donuts (or doughnuts), but this version can satisfy your cravings with a healthy alternative. The double dose of chocolate will fulfil your chocoholic desires, and the rose petal topping makes it ever so feminine.

Yield: 8 donuts
Total Time: 1 hour 15 minutes
Equipment: Food processor, mixing bowls, large pan, nonstick donut pan, silicone spatula, piping tip (Wilton 1M or your choice), piping bags.

FLAVOURS: Lots of rich sweet chocolate taste in the donut and frosting. The addition of rose extract offsets the rich chocolate and brings a unique flavour combination you are unlikely to forget.

BENEFITS: Baking instead of frying lowers the saturated fat content. Replacing refined sugar with applesauce decreases calories and eliminates empty carbohydrates. The sweet potatoes add fibre, protein, vitamin A, vitamin C and magnesium. It's almost like being rewarded for eating donuts!

DONUTS

¾ cup (90 g) whole wheat pastry flour or (60 g all-purpose flour and 30 g whole wheat flour)

¼ cup (20 g) unsweetened cocoa powder

1 tsp baking powder

pinch of salt

¾ cup (185 g) applesauce (see page 204)

¾ cup (230 g) date purée (see page 208)

¼ cup (60 ml) unsweetened plant milk (almond, walnut, soy, etc.)

1 tsp vanilla extract or rose extract

CHOCOLATE FROSTING

½ cup (100 g) sweet potato purée (see page 213)

¼ cup (77 g) date purée (see page 208)

2 tbsp (32 g) almond butter

5 tbsp (38 g) unsweetened cocoa

¼ medium (30 g) avocado

1 tbsp (15 ml) filtered water

¼ tsp monk fruit or ½ cup (100 g) sugar or maple syrup

1 tbsp (9 g) date sugar (add more if desired)

DONUT

Preheat oven to 350°F (177°C).

Mix dry ingredients in a medium mixing bowl. Mix wet ingredients in another bowl.

Add wet ingredients into dry ingredients. Mix just until combined.

Pipe the batter into the wells of the donut pan. Fill pretty close to the top. Smooth the batter. Tap once to get the air bubbles out.

Bake for 12–18 minutes or until the donuts spring back. Do not overbake.

Cool donuts for a few minutes before releasing from the pan. They should come out easily. Use silicone or plastic spatula to release, so that you don't damage your nonstick pan surface.

CHOCOLATE FROSTING

While the donuts are baking, put all frosting ingredients in a food processor and blend until creamy (60-90 seconds). Check for taste and sweetness and adjust as desired.

When donuts are cool, put a piping tip into a piping bag and fill halfway with frosting. Frost each donut. Add edible rose petals and blossoms and other decorations as you wish.

Note: This frosting will yield about 9–10 servings, so you will have some leftover depending on how you frost the donuts.

Thank you to *The China Study Family Cookbook* for inspiration for this recipe adapted and reprinted with permission from the T. Colin Campbell Center for Nutrition Studies (nutritionstudies.org).

NUTRITION: *(per serving)*
1 frosted donut, 2½ oz (75 g)
monk fruit | sugar

Calories	197	235
Fat	4.5 g
Saturated Fat	0.8 g
Cholesterol	0 mg
Carbohydrate	39.1 g	50 g
Fibre	6.9 g
Protein	4.3 g
Sugar	22.1 g	32 g
Sodium	39 mg

Candied fruit and vegetables at Les Halles de Lyon Paul Bocuse market

Lyon

THE CAPITAL OF FRENCH CUISINE

View of Lyon looking east from La Basilique Notre-Dame de Fourvière

Les Mères de Lyon

THE MOTHERS OF LYON

Located in east-central France, Lyon is the country's third-largest city, after Paris and Marseille. Founded over 2,000 years ago as the Roman fort Lugdunum, it is an important economic and social hub. A wide variety of large commercial businesses, international institutions and arts organisations make the city their headquarters.

But I am not in Lyon for these reasons. I'm here for the beautiful sights, food and the ingenious women who lie behind its reputation as one of the world's great food capitals.

"The Weight of Oneself" statue near the Lyon Court of Appeals

The walk up to the La Basilique Notre-Dame de Fourvière

Strolling along the banks of the River Saône

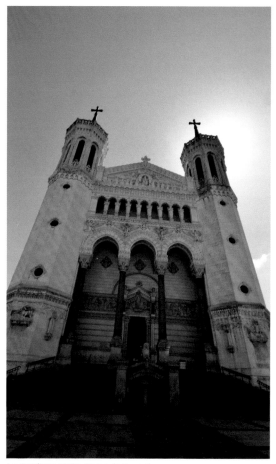

La Basilique Notre-Dame de Fourvière

My hotel is well-situated in the 6th Arrondissement (district) near the Rhône River and a beautiful park named Tête d'Or. I've found that the best way to get to know a place is to walk. Not only is it good exercise, but it's slow enough to get to know the sounds, smells and visual details of a place. And it's a great way to build an appetite.

There are so many great walks, winding and narrow side streets and quaint shops in Lyon. I spend a couple of hours traversing central Lyon, including bridges across the Rhône and the Saône Rivers, gradually making my way up steep streets to the outlook at La Basilique Notre-Dame de Fourvière. The views are beautiful, and the basilica is very striking.

I'm going to splurge on lunch today at La Mère Brazier, a two-star Michelin restaurant, and share a story about the women behind the food of Lyon, as well as the rise of French cuisine and its journey into kitchens across the world.

Enterprising Women

WHO TURNED ADVERSITY INTO SUSTENANCE

In the 18th and 19th centuries, Lyon was an important industrial centre, particularly for silk manufacturing. Wealthy families often employed women to be their personal chefs, but there were economic downturns during this period, which meant that many families were no longer able to employ these women. So what did they do with their cooking skills?

They set up small restaurants, or bouchons, where men working in factories could eat large often pork-based meals, accompanied by local wine, at a reasonable price. This formed the basis of traditional Lyonnaise cuisine.

Many women emerged from this culinary tradition, taking French cuisine to the next level in terms of quality and celebrity. They include la Mère Guy, la Mère Fillioux, la Mère Brazier and la Mère Léa.

Lovely flowers in Lyon's Tête d'Or park – France's largest municipal park

"This exceptional woman... taught all of us about flavours and gave us a taste for hard work and work well done. There would have been no success for any of us without her."

Quote attributed to Paul Bocuse concerning Eugénie Brazier

La Mère Brazier

Eugénie Brazier

La Mère Brazier restaurant

One of the trailblazers of French cuisine, Eugénie Brazier, known as "la Mère Brazier" (1895 – 1977), grew up in an impoverished farming family. When she was ten years old, her mother died. She was sent to live with another farm family. Her formal schooling was limited to two months a year. At 19, she had a child out of wedlock, Gaston, and began working and cooking for a wealthy Lyon merchant. Eventually, she left to join la Mère Fillioux where she built her culinary skills. In 1921, at age 26, she opened her first restaurant, La Mère Brazier, in the 1st Arrondissement, Lyon. Starting out, her funds were so limited that one supplier allowed her to return unsold ingredients after the night's dinner.

She later bought a bungalow on Col de la Luère, Pollionnay and converted it into a restaurant. Both her establishments won three Michelin stars. She became the first restaurateur with six Michelin stars in France – male or female. Her style was extremely modest relative to her accomplishments. The current La Mère Brazier restaurant in Lyon has achieved two Michelin stars with chef Mathieu Viannay. A highlight of my meal was the *artichaut foie gras* (artichoke with duck pâté). *Parfait*.

Madame Brazier's version of cuisine classique became famous with politicians and celebrities, including famous novelist and food critic Prince Curnonsky. She helped to train the next generation of chefs, including Paul Bocuse (1926 – 2018), whose career exemplified the rise of nouvelle cuisine, a leaner version of classic French cuisine, and the emergence of the celebrity chef.

So far on our journey through France, we have met the Widows of Champagne and the Mothers of Lyon. They all strived for the highest standards and flavours. This is the spirit of Flavour with Benefits!

Shopping for fresh vegetables at Les Halles de Lyon Paul Bocuse

Pont de la Feuillée bridge over the River Saône in Lyon

A Visual Feast

SHOPPING IN A FRENCH MARKET

No visit to Lyon would be complete without a visit to the local markets. I'm going to the covered market – Les Halles de Lyon Paul Bocuse. I love the quality and freshness of the ingredients. The strawberries are the best I've ever tasted. People tend to shop more often here, so the food is fresher and the flavours are more intense.

There are also strict European regulations against genetic modification. This means the actual integrity of the food is intact and has not been altered to ward off insects and become resistant to pesticides. The produce has more flavour and is healthier too.

Cheese shop at Les Halles de Lyon Paul Bocuse

Lyon side street

Recipes + Flavours Inspired

BY LES MÈRES DE LYON

In honour of Les Mères de Lyon, I've created some desserts, one of which is a touch erotic! Who says you can't have dessert first? Then onto the rest of the meal, with some healthy alternatives for entrées and soups.

TÉTONS DE VÉNUS CAKES

Innovation was key to thriving in Lyon in the 1800s, so "la Mère Brigousse" had an idea: make cakes for bachelor parties. They were called *Tétons de Vénus* or Breasts of Venus. With history in mind, my recipe is inspired by this original cake and a recognition of breast health awareness. This treat is complex and takes some time because it is four recipes in one: chocolate mousse, vanilla cake for the "breasts", sponge cake for the base and a white chocolate glaze. This is not health food; it's fun food!

Yield: 8 cakes
Total Time: 2–3 hours
Equipment: Mixer, small silicone round candy moulds, spherical cake moulds, silicone mat, 13" x 9" (33 cm x 23 cm) sheet cake pan, candy thermometer, cooling racks, cookie cutters, cake boards

FLAVOURS: These cakes are filled with chocolate mousse and have a lovely vanilla cake on the outside. They are finished with a decadent white chocolate glaze, which gives them a festive shimmer in the light. Topped off with the anatomical suggestion of a nipple, the blueberry adds some fun.

BENEFITS: The pure fun of a chocolate-filled cake! Using avocado as the base of the chocolate filling lowers saturated fats and adds B vitamins and vitamin K. Carob adds necessary calcium. And since these are a sexy treat, why not improve sexual vitality with red maca, grown especially for female fertility.

CHOCOLATE MOUSSE

1 ripe avocado (130 g)

¼ cup (30 g) finest cocoa

2 tbsp (13 g) toasted carob powder

¼ tsp monk fruit or ½ cup (100 g) sugar

¼ cup (34 g) date sugar

2 tsp red maca powder

CHOCOLATE MOUSSE

Mix ingredients in a food processor for 45–60 seconds or until smooth. Taste for sweetness and adjust as needed.

Use a small spatula to press the mixture into silicone candy moulds. Fill the moulds to the top and smooth them with the spatula.

Place in the freezer for 1 hour or longer, until needed.

VANILLA CAKE

8 tbsp (113 g) unsalted butter

¼ tsp monk fruit or 1 cup (200 g) sugar

2 tbsp (30 ml) canola oil

2 large eggs

2 tbsp (26 ml) vanilla extract

1½ cups (180 g) cake flour, sifted

½ tsp baking soda

¾ cup (182 ml) whole milk

1 tsp apple cider vinegar

SPONGE CAKE BASE

2 large eggs, separated, at room temperature

¼ cup (50 g) granulated sugar, divided in half

1 tbsp (15 ml) milk (or nondairy milk)

¼ tsp almond extract

¼ cup plus 2 tbsp (40 g) cake flour

2 tbsp (15 g) almond flour

¼ tsp fine sea salt

VANILLA CAKE

Preheat oven to 350°F (177°C) and spray the spherical cake moulds. Take the chocolate mousse out of the freezer.

In a small bowl, beat sugar or monk fruit with butter until smooth. Add eggs and vanilla and beat with a mixer or a whisk until well combined.

In a small bowl, whisk together flour, salt and baking soda. Add half of this dry mixture to the wet ingredients and beat for 5 seconds. Stir in half of the milk and mix thoroughly. Add the vinegar and mix until smooth. Then add the rest of the dry ingredients and beat well. Finally, add the rest of the milk. Mix until smooth.

Add cake batter to each cavity until it is half full. Gently remove the chocolate mousse pieces from the silicone moulds and place one in each cavity of the cake mould. Press to the bottom of the batter.

Add more batter to each cavity until they are three-quarters full. The baked cake may rise over the top slightly, but can be trimmed.

Bake for 25 minutes or until done. Press lightly to see if they spring back.

SPONGE CAKE BASE

Oven should still be at 350°F (177°C).

Line the sheet pan with aluminum foil or a silicone baking mat. Grease or butter only the foil, if used. Cake will not stick to silicone.

Place egg yolks in a bowl and whisk vigorously with 3 tablespoons of sugar until light in colour. Whisk in milk and almond extract.

Sift in the cake flour and almond flour. Add salt and fold in until just incorporated. Set batter aside.

In a medium bowl, whip egg whites with a mixer on high speed until frothy. Add remaining 1 tablespoon sugar and beat until whites hold medium peaks.

Fold one-third of the egg whites into the batter mixture, then place the batter mixture into the bowl with the egg whites, folding until just incorporated and no white streaks remain.

Pour batter into prepared sheet pan and spread it into a thin, even layer.

Bake for 9–11 minutes or until the cake is spongy to the touch and barely starting to darken around the edges. Let cool completely.

When cool, cut out 8 circles with a cookie cutter or small bowl for the base of the vanilla cakes. Put a cooling rack on top of a pan and put one sponge cake bottom layer under each vanilla cake. Put pan of assembled cakes into the freezer. They should freeze for at least 30 minutes, but an hour is better. This will help the glaze stick to them.

MIRROR GLAZE

MIRROR GLAZE
6 sheets leaf gelatin (not powdered gelatin)
1 cup (200 g) sugar
⅔ cup (225 ml) light corn syrup
½ cup (118 ml) water
½ cup (118 ml) sweetened condensed milk
1 cup (198 g) good quality white chocolate, finely chopped
1-2 tsp gel or powder food colouring

NUTRITION: *(per serving)*
1 cake, 11 ounces (315 g)

Calories	691
Fat	28.7 g
Saturated Fat	12.8 g
Cholesterol	129 mg
Carbohydrate	104.9 g
Fibre	3.7 g
Protein	9.1 g
Sugar	66.4 g
Sodium	280 mg

MIRROR GLAZE

Cut gelatin into 1-inch strips and submerge in cool water for at least 5 minutes to soften. Place white chocolate in a heat-proof bowl and set aside. Squeeze out as much water as possible once they are softened.

Combine sugar, corn syrup, and water in a saucepan and bring to a boil over medium heat until sugar is completely dissolved and mixture is clear.

Remove from heat, then add gelatin and whisk until dissolved. Whisk in sweetened condensed milk. Pour the hot mixture over chopped white chocolate and let sit for 30 seconds.

Stir until chocolate is completely melted and mixture is smooth.

Let glaze cool, stirring occasionally, until glaze reaches approximately 95°F (35°C) on an instant-read thermometer. The glaze needs to be the correct temperature, or it will not form a thick enough layer on the outside of the cakes.

When the glaze reaches 95–96°F (35°C), add powder or gel food colouring as desired. Darker colours tend to look beautiful with this glaze technique. You can also divide your glaze into multiple colours and then swirl them if you'd like.

Remove assembled cakes from freezer with the cooling rack still in place. This will allow easy clean-up when the glaze is poured over the cakes. Make sure they are not touching to ensure the glaze is evenly spread over each cake.

You may also want to cut out small rounds of cardboard to place under each cake to make them easier to transfer.

Pour glaze generously over cakes, taking care to ensure there are no bare spots left. Allow the excess glaze to drip off for 5 or 10 minutes, then gently scrape the edges to remove any remaining drops. Put blueberries and other decorations on the tops of the breast cakes right after pouring the glaze to make sure they stick.

Carefully transfer cakes using a small offset spatula to the cardboard cake rounds or small pieces of parchment paper for easy movement.

Any leftover glaze can be scraped up and refrigerated in an airtight container for later use.

Glazed cakes will keep in the refrigerator for up to 5 days. Let them rise to room temperature before serving.

FESTIVE BEAUJOLAIS POACHED PEARS

These are a lovely dessert for parties or special occasion. They are easy to make and will add a wow factor to your next party, without too much work.

FLAVOURS: The pears and wine are satisfying and aromatic. The crystallised ginger adds some heat and sweetness, making this dessert satisfying for all the senses.

BENEFITS: It is vegan, gluten-free and fairly fast to make. As a source of vitamin C and copper, it assists the immune system. Boasting a high-fibre content, it is great substitute for less healthy options.

Yield: 4 pears
Total Time: 1 hour (not including making crystallised ginger)
Equipment: Saucepan, vegetable peeler, slotted spoon

2 cups (453 ml) Beaujolais red wine

1 tsp monk fruit or ⅓ cup (67 g) sugar

1 cup (237 ml) filtered water

4 cinnamon sticks (extra for garnish for serving)

1 tbsp (14 ml) lemon juice

12 pieces crystallised ginger (125 g), 2" x 2" (5 cm–7 cm) lengths (see page 207)

4 medium Bosc pears (716 g)

¼–½ cup (118 ml) ginger/sugar water (see page 207)

Combine the red wine, water, cinnamon sticks, lemon juice, monk fruit (or sugar) and ginger in a medium saucepan. Bring to a boil, stirring constantly. Lower the heat and maintain a rolling simmer.

Peel the pears carefully to try to have as smooth a surface as possible. Trim the stamen on the bottom of the pear if it is too prominent.

Using a slotted spoon, place the pears carefully into the wine syrup mixture. If there is not enough liquid to cover them, gently baste them with syrup from time to time. It is best to poach 2 pears at a time. You can turn them but be careful not to bruise them. Poach for 15–18 minutes.

Use the slotted spoon to remove pears from the wine syrup and set aside. Increase heat to high and boil poaching liquid to reduce to three-quarters. It should be a fairly thick syrup.

Drizzle the poached pears with the thickened wine syrup and ginger/water and serve with other garnishes such the cooked cinnamon sticks or coconut whipped cream if desired.

NUTRITION: *(per serving)*

1 pear, sugar | monk fruit	
Calories	170 | 145
Fat	0.3 g
Saturated Fat	0 g
Cholesterol	0 mg
Carbohydrate	34 g | 28 g
Fibre	5.8 g
Protein	0.8 g
Sugar	21 g | 17.8 g
Sodium	19 mg

CHOCOLATE MOUSSE – AVOCADO SURPRISE

Don't tell your guests what the main ingredient is. Leave them guessing. The velvety creaminess of this mousse is lovely, and when they learn that it's avocado, it will be a pleasant surprise. For beautiful presentation, serve it with plant-based whipped cream. This one's a crowd-pleaser!

Yield: 1 cup, 2 servings
Total Time: 15 minutes
Equipment: Food processor, spatula and piping bag with tip

2 ripe avocados (265 g)

½ cup (50 g) unsweetened natural cocoa

2 tbsp (17 g) toasted carob powder

1 tsp monk fruit or
1 cup (120 g) icing sugar

¼ cup (34 g) date sugar or
¼ cup (63 g) white sugar

2 tsp red maca powder

½ cup (63 g) fresh raspberries (for garnish when serving)

coconut whipped cream

FLAVOURS: The surprising creamy texture and rich chocolate flavour is offset by the naturally sweet taste of fresh raspberries.

BENEFITS: This healthy mousse is 50% lower in calories and saturated fat and has no cholesterol. The raspberries add vitamin C, fibre, and even manganese, which regulates blood sugar and lowers inflammation. The other ingredient to mention is red maca. In addition to its many nutrients, it is said to improve sex drive, fertility and mood. Oh là là! Now we're talking "Flavour with Benefits"! Further personal study on these claims is recommended and government grants are not required!

Place all ingredients (up to the maca powder) in a food processor and blend until smooth.

Taste for sweetness and adjust as needed with additional date or refined sugar.

Pipe onto dishes or scoop out with a spoon. Garnish with raspberries and coconut whipped cream.

NUTRITION: *(per serving)*
¼ cup (94 g),
monk fruit + date sugar | sugar

Calories	133 | 191
Fat	10.5 g | 10.6 g
Saturated Fat	2.5 g
Cholesterol	0 mg
Carbohydrate	11.8 g | 26.8 g
Fibre	5.4 g
Protein	2.1 g
Sugar	4.4 g | 19.1 g
Sodium	5 mg

Sometimes you stumble on exciting information when you research the past. It turns out that crêpes date back to the mid-13th century. The original name was Crespes (crisp), and like a lot of inventions, these came about when something unintentional happened – like pouring porridge onto a hot griddle. The recipe I found, merely gave instructions with no measurements. It reminded me of my maternal grandmother's "recipes".

But Medievalcuisine.com took the time to figure out the details, and it interested me because it was naturally leavened, which makes sense in a Medieval recipe. The original flour was buckwheat, an ancient grain, so they are gluten-free too. You'll find that these crêpes are lacy and light. The challenge was making them oil-free and vegan – and it worked beautifully. One is never enough!

FLAVOURS: The buckwheat gives a silky, nutty taste, paired with the sweetness of ripe pears and raspberries, topped off with cinnamon and maple syrup. The coconut yoghurt filling is cool with a complex taste. Need we say more?

BENEFITS: This breakfast, lunch or dinner crêpe is packed with calcium, B vitamins and minerals such as manganese. With no cholesterol, it is healthy and versatile.

Yield: 8–9 medium sized crêpes
Total Time: 2 hours 45 minutes
Equipment: Nonstick pan, preferably a lightweight crêpe pan, mixing bowl, silicone spatula, ¼ cup measuring cup

CRÊPE

2 flax "eggs" (see note)

1¾ cups less 1 tbsp (227 g) buckwheat flour

pinch of salt, optional

¾ cup (168 ml) white wine

1 cup (237 ml) filtered water

FILLING & SERVING SUGGESTIONS

3 tbsp plant-based yoghurt, piped inside and on the edge

drizzle maple syrup

6 or more strawberries, sliced

½ pear, sliced

cinnamon for dusting

Mix all the crêpe ingredients in a mixing bowl and stir until combined. Cover the bowl and put in a warm place for 2 hours.

After 2 hours, depending on the quality and age of the buckwheat flour, it should look like a typical pancake batter and be pourable. If the batter is too thick, thin it out first with ¼ cup of water. If it is still too thick, add ¼ cup more water and mix thoroughly. This should be sufficient.

To cook, heat up a nonstick pan, preferably a crêpe pan over medium heat. You should not need any oil. Hold the pan at about a 45-degree angle and pour ¼ cup of batter onto the pan. If the pan is hot enough, it will not spill out. Swirl as much as possible and then set back onto the heat. The first side should cook in 2 minutes or so. When all the wet spots are cooked, and the edges slightly lift up, this side is done.

Place your spatula carefully under the edge of the crêpe and slide it underneath. Flip it over. Cook for 1–2 more minutes. You should see steam bubbles. When it is no longer steaming, the crêpe is done. It should look lacy on the flipped side. Place this side on top when serving. Do not overcook or they will be tough. There are no eggs, so there are no health concerns from undercooking.

Serve immediately with pears and strawberries. Fill with coconut yoghurt and dust with cinnamon.

Note: In a small bowl, add 2 tablespoons of ground flaxseed (preferably golden flaxseed) and mix with 6 tablespoons of warm water. Let sit for five minutes, until it has a gel-like consistency.

NUTRITION: *(per serving)*
1 crêpe (no toppings or fillings)

Calories	140
Fat	1.5 g
Saturated Fat	0 g
Cholesterol	0 mg
Carbohydrate	23 g
Fibre	6.7 g
Protein	3.5 g
Sugar	2.4g
Sodium	27mg

PEAR RASPBERRY QUINOA SALAD WITH AGED BALSAMIC VINEGAR

After all these desserts, sometimes we may want salad as a main meal. This one fills the bill. The addition of quinoa adds protein and healthy carbohydrates to keep you full longer. This salad is easy and fast to make. Just use what you find in the refrigerator. It can be made ahead, too.

FLAVOURS: The combination of raspberries, pears, lettuce, kale, quinoa, carrots, sweet potatoes and red potatoes brings a blend of sweet and savoury flavours. Every bite is a surprise.

BENEFITS: The rainbow of fruits, vegetables and cremini mushrooms provides protein, fibre and a variety of vitamins and minerals. The salad is also low-calorie, so you can eat as much as you want. The added bonus of an oil-free dressing is a reduction in calories from fat.

Yield: 1.3 kg serves 12+
Total Time: 15 minutes
Equipment: Pot, sharp knife

Mix all the ingredients in a large bowl.

Toss and serve with regular or white balsamic vinegar.

Add salt and pepper to taste. This can be stored in a resealable container without the dressing and it will keep for several days.

½ cup (96 g) cooked quinoa

1 cup (150 g) red onion, diced

1 cup (200 g) tomatoes, diced

¾ cup (90 g) cremini mushrooms, diced

1 cup (40 g) spring mix salad (pre-washed)

¾ cup (100 g) kale salad mix (pre-washed)

1 cup (100 g) celery, diced

⅓ cup (50 g) carrots, diced

⅔ cup (150 g) red potatoes, cubed

⅔ cup (135 g) sweet potatoes, cubed

⅔ cup (100 g) pear, cubed

⅔ cup (85 g) raspberries or blueberries

½ cup (50 g) cashews or pumpkin seeds, crushed

white or regular balsamic vinegar

NUTRITION: *(per serving)*
2¾ cup (100 g)

Calories	66
Fat	1.8 g
Saturated Fat	0.3 g
Cholesterol	0 mg
Carbohydrate	10.9 g
Fibre	1.9 g
Protein	2.4 g
Sugar	1.9 g
Sodium	13 mg

CAULIFLOWER STEAK ON CAULIFLOWER POTATO SOUP

Roasted cauliflower steak on spicy soup is an elegant meal for all occasions. Use one cauliflower to make both the soup and the steaks. With no added oil, this low-calorie superfood is high in antioxidants and fibre, and it's a dish that everyone will love.

FLAVOURS: The satisfying crunch of grilled cauliflower paired with puréed cauliflower and baked potato make this meal light and sophisticated. The turmeric and curry powder give it colour and spice. Combined with the roasted garlic, onions and herbs, this soup will bring comfort on a cold day.

BENEFITS: With no oil used in roasting, the fat content is low. The cauliflower is packed with B vitamins, potassium, calcium, vitamin K (good for blood clotting and bone health) and of course, fibre. Potatoes with the skins on add key minerals such as phosphorus.

Yield: 2 large servings
Total Time: 1 hour 30 minutes
Equipment: Food processor, large pot, cast-iron pan, sharp knife, small bowl, tongs

SOUP

1 cauliflower (about 575 g), end trimmed

2 baked potatoes (150 g), skins on

4½ tbsp (70 g) onions, minced

3 cups (700 ml) no sodium vegetable broth

2 tsp white miso bean paste

1 tsp tamari

2 tsp fresh rosemary, minced

1 tsp curry powder

½ tsp coriander powder

½ tsp dried thyme

½ tsp turmeric powder

3-4 roasted garlic cloves, diced

½ tsp harissa pepper (optional)

ground pepper to taste

pinch of sea salt (optional)

Italian parsley for garnish

Preheat oven to 450°F (232°C).

Stand the cauliflower up on its stalk. Cut it vertically to make two 1-inch (3 cm) slices from the middle. Set the two large centre pieces aside for the steaks. The rest of the cauliflower will be used for the soup.

SOUP
Take the smaller outer cauliflower pieces, break up the florets and place them into the food processor along with the potatoes. Purée for about 45 seconds or until smooth. Put into a large pot.

Add the broth and the rest of the ingredients into the pot and cook on medium-high heat. Once the soup is softly boiling, turn down the heat to medium-low to keep at a simmer. Cook for 30–45 minutes with the lid partially on. Stir occasionally. The soup should be thick enough to support the steaks when they are placed on top.

CAULIFLOWER STEAKS

2 steak slices (about 150–160 g each)

1 tsp almond or cashew butter

1 tbsp (15 ml) water

CAULIFLOWER STEAKS
Put the cast-iron pan in the middle rack of the preheated oven for about 10 minutes. Mix the nut butter and water together until thoroughly mixed.

Spread the mixture onto the hot cast-iron pan. The pan should sizzle.

Place the two steak slices into the hot pan with tongs. The steaks should not be touching each other.

Bake for 10–15 minutes on each side. Carefully turn them over with the tongs. They should start to brown, but be careful not to burn them.

For additional browning, broil at 550°F (288°C) for 2–3 minutes on each side. Watch carefully as they will burn quickly. Ladle the soup into two bowls and carefully place each steak on the soup. They should not sink into the soup. Garnish with Italian parsley. Serve hot.

NUTRITION: *(per serving)*
1 bowl + 1 steak

Calories	243
Fat	1.3 g
Saturated Fat	0.2 g
Cholesterol	0 mg
Carbohydrate	53.8 g
Fibre	11.5 g
Protein	10.7 g
Sugar	10.8 g
Sodium	127 mg

FRENCH POTATO SALAD

This potato salad is a tasty, affordable side-dish, or an essential part of Salad Niçoise (see page 164). It is tangy and spicy. Best of all, no peeling the potatoes. Leave the skins on. They have most of the nutrition. Fresh and dried herbs, with vinegar and lemon juice, will dress up the often-overlooked potato.

Yield: 24 oz (680 g), serves 4
Total Time: 40 minutes
Equipment: Large pot, sharp knife, mixing bowl

FLAVOURS: Fragrant rosemary, tarragon, thyme, dill and sage balance the tangy vinegar and the Dijon mustard, with potatoes as the backdrop.

BENEFITS: Boiled or baked potatoes with the skins on are loaded with fibre, vitamins C and B6 and have more potassium than a banana.

POTATOES

3 pounds (1.36 kg) small red or white potatoes, washed and skin on, thickly sliced

DRESSING

¼ cup (80 ml) filtered water

3 tbsp (22 ml) lemon juice

½ lemon, zested

1 tbsp (14 ml) apple cider vinegar

1 tbsp (14 ml) white wine vinegar

2 tsp stone ground mustard or Dijon mustard

4 cloves of garlic, pressed

1 tsp sea salt or tamari

1 tsp ground black pepper

3–4 tbsp (18 g) fresh herbs (such as rosemary, French tarragon, thyme, dill, sage, marjoram)

½ small red onion (50 g) or 1 shallot, finely diced

8 cherry tomatoes (114 g), sliced for garnish

POTATOES

Boil the sliced potatoes in a large pot. Add enough water to submerge all the potatoes. Cover and bring to a boil. Reduce to a simmer and continue cooking until they are fork-tender, about 10–15 minutes. Test after 10 minutes. Do not overcook.

Drain the potatoes and let cool for about 15–20 minutes. While the potatoes are cooling, make the dressing.

DRESSING

Mix or whisk water, lemon juice, lemon zest, vinegars, stone ground mustard, pressed garlic, salt or tamari and ground black pepper in a small mixing bowl until well combined. Pour dressing mixture over potatoes and slightly mix to moisten all potatoes. Add the fresh herbs and diced onions or shallots and toss the potatoes gently. Season with additional salt and pepper as needed. Ideally, cover and chill in the refrigerator for an hour. Serve chilled with sliced cherry tomatoes as a garnish.

NUTRITION: *(per serving)*
6 oz (170 g)

Calories	168
Fat	0.5 g
Saturated Fat	0.1 g
Cholesterol	0 mg
Carbohydrate	37.9 g
Fibre	3.8 g
Protein	3.9 g
Sugar	1.8 g
Sodium	111 mg

FANCY PIPED SWEET POTATOES

These sweet potatoes are baked to perfection, then mashed and piped. A few fancy touches make this a great side dish at a party. Those who are reluctant to eat vegetables might find this irresistible. Sweet potatoes are one of the most nutritious and popular foods on earth, with 1,000s of varieties available.

FLAVOURS: The natural sweetness of the sweet potatoes and the delicious pumpkin pie spices make this dish feel like dessert.

BENEFITS: Sweet potatoes are low in calories, high in protein, manganese and fibre. They are loaded with vitamins A and C, both of which help with a healthy immune system. The natural sweetness and aromatic spices will satisfy your sweet tooth.

Yield: 4 servings
Total Time: 45 minutes
Equipment: Sharp knife, roasting pan, parchment paper, piping bag or a resealable plastic bag, Wilton 1M piping tip

2 orange sweet potatoes (227 g)

2 white or other colour sweet potatoes (227 g)

¼ tsp vanilla extract

2 tsp cinnamon

1 tsp nutmeg or mace

½ tsp ground ginger (optional)

¼ cup (18 g) slivered blanched almonds

Preheat oven to 425°F (218°C).

Wash the sweet potatoes and cut out any bad spots. No peeling required.

Bake for 30–40 minutes depending on the shape of the sweet potatoes. They should be fork-tender.

Mash the sweet potatoes in a bowl and add the spices. Mix thoroughly. Serve with a spoon or, for a nice touch, place the sweet potato mash into a piping bag or resealable plastic bag and pipe out a design on each serving plate. Sprinkle with more cinnamon (you can never have enough!) and sliced almonds on top. Serve immediately. If they have cooled off too much, put them in the microwave for 20 seconds.

NUTRITION: *(per serving)*
½ cup (100 g)

Calories	119
Fat	0.3 g
Saturated Fat	0.2 g
Cholesterol	0 mg
Carbohydrate	27.6 g
Fibre	4.7g
Protein	2.1 g
Sugar	5.7 g
Sodium	72 mg

View of Les Baux-de-Provence, Provence, France

Meandering

THROUGH PROVENCE

Arles

COBBLED SIDE STREETS AND QUIET MOMENTS

We are leaving the delicacies of Lyon behind and heading to the southern region of France, known as Provence.

When you think of Provence, what first comes to mind? Fields of lavender? *A Year in Provence* by Peter Mayle? The Cannes Film Festival? The colour yellow?

Well, yes, Provence is known for many things. Incredible scenery. Outstanding food and many local festivals. The French Riviera. My first Provençal destination will be the ancient city of Arles, known for its Roman ruins and being an artists' enclave.

I'm staying in the old city in a renovated apartment about 100 metres from the Rhône River. The apartment has a well-outfitted kitchen so I can have some culinary fun, and there is a fourth-floor terrace to survey local rooftops and cathedral steeples.

The small, crooked side streets are covered with cobblestones and countless drains to handle the spring storms brought by the most southerly of the mistral winds. A variety of flowering vines soften the patchwork of stone and brick façades of the small homes.

Dutch artist Vincent van Gogh painted over 200 works of art in Provence in over 15 months, and it was also here that he lost an ear. Pablo Picasso painted several portraits of his first wife, Olga Khokhlova, dressed in local Arlesian costumes. Popular tourist sites are everywhere, including the 2,000-year-old Roman amphitheatre and Roman baths.

I can understand why artists come here. The atmosphere, the sunlight, the rosé wine. I believe this would be an excellent place to write a book!

I'll have a chance to pick up some fresh fruits and vegetables, including lemons and culinary lavender. I'll use them with the items I purchased in Lyon to create some unique meals and desserts inspired by the quiet beauty of this ancient city.

Street corner "lookout" statue and symbols

Beautiful flowers are everywhere in Provence

Romantic side streets in old Arles

Arles city streets and outdoor cafés

Panorama of Rue Croix Rouge (Red Cross Road) in old Arles leading to the Rhône River

The Arles Roman Amphitheatre, built in 90 AD, can seat 20,000 people and once hosted chariot races and gladiator battles. Today it hosts bullfighting.

Typical houses in old Arles

Arles side street

Let's see what's at the top of the hill ....

Les Alpilles

(THE MINI ALPS)
VISIT TO LES BAUX-DE-PROVENCE

Arles is located near the mouth of the Rhône River (Bouches-du-Rhône). It is ideally situated for short day tours into other wonderful places, such as the Camargue, Avignon, Aix-en-Provence and Les Alpilles.

Today, I have a little extra time, and I'm going into Les Alpilles (the mini Alps) to visit Château des Baux-de-Provence, the spectacular ruins of the fortified castle situated on a rocky outcrop. The castle dates back to the 8th century.

A stone stairway that leads to an intriguing collection of walled houses, twisting alleyways and outlooks catches my attention. There is so much to explore here. The majestic rocks take your breath away.

At the top of the hill, I come to a plateau and cliff with sweeping views of the surrounding valley with fertile olive orchards, vineyards and rock faces. I linger awhile. Time slows. What a luxury! I need to come back and stay for more than a day.

.... a stunning valley view from the cliffs around the Baux valley

View from Château des Baux-de-Provence

Ruins and alleyways at Château des Baux-de-Provence

Café and shops at Château des Baux-de-Provence

Vincent was Right

IT IS ABOUT THE LIGHT

"There is a sun, a light that for want of another word I can only call yellow, pale sulphur yellow, pale golden citron. How lovely yellow is!"

Vincent van Gogh

Vincent was onto something. The quality of the light in Provence is both alluring and comforting. In French, *la lumière à la fois séduisante et réconfortante*. Oh my, I'm feeling a little warm.

With all the incredible ingredients available in Provence for lovely salads and desserts, I am feeling hungry. I'm sure Vincent would have liked some desserts made in his honour. Let me present them to you.

The first one is a pie rendition of his *The Starry Night* painting. He painted this masterpiece in June 1889. It portrays the view from his room at the asylum in Saint-Rémy-de-Provence, just before sunrise.

The second dessert is a Provençale cheesecake that has both lemon and lavender. How is that for allure and comfort? Hmm, I like that. Ready to surrender to the light?

The yellow is for Vincent. The desserts are for you.

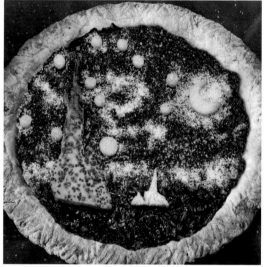

Tribute to Vincent Van Gogh: The Starry Night Maple Blueberry Deep-Dish Pie (page 140)

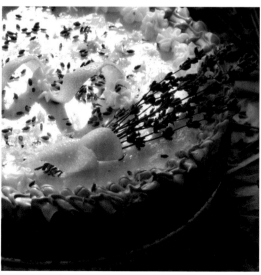

Lemon Lavender Luxury Cheesecake (page 145)

Let's Disappear

IN THE CAMARGUE TO A SECRET GARDEN

Just a little south of Arles is the mysterious marsh area known as the Camargue. It is approximately 100,000 hectares (240,000 acres) and is framed by two arms of the Rhône River pushing out into the Mediterranean. It is well-known for its birds, particularly flamingos, and its wild white horses and black bulls.

I am heading to a restaurant, La Chassagnette, for lunch and some sightseeing. I drive with the windows down. The sun feels warm and comforting. The air is heavy with humidity and smells sweet. Tall grasses sway in the breeze. The roads take gentle turns along fields of red rice, lined with wildflowers. I am so lost in the moment that I forget my turnoff. As I head back, I spot some of the white horses the area is famous for.

Camargue horses

Fresh produce ready for my meal at La Chassagnette restaurant

The garden of La Chassagnette restaurant

More garden views at the restaurant

Heading out to explore

La Chassagnette is in the heart of the Rhône River delta and features a glorious flower garden surrounded by organic produce. There are over 200 different types of vegetables, herbs and fruits grown across two hectares on the site. I stop in the middle of the garden and sit on one of the benches and close my eyes. The background of a gurgling fountain and the hum of industrious bees provide a rare calm. What a glorious place!

The next thing I know, someone is gently touching my shoulder. "Madame, your table is ready." I don't know about you, but that is a great phrase to wake up to!

The restaurant's menu is based on what is in season in their garden and the local markets. It has a well-earned Michelin star for chef Armand Arnal and this labour of love.

I choose a five-course menu that takes me on a tour of spring produce. The ingredients are freshly picked and beautifully presented. I'm not sure about which dessert to choose. They all sound so marvellous. I let the waiter know that I'll make that choice a little later.

This is the ideal meal. Thoughtfully prepared food in a lovely setting, with local ingredients and pleasant company. My favourite place to eat is at home with family and friends. Laughter, smiles, thoughts shared and memories made. But this restaurant has a unique *ambiance*. Beautiful light. Happy customers. Delicious food. Attentive staff.

There's a couple sitting at the next table, and by the sound of their conversation, they're celebrating something. Periodically, they lean over and kiss. It's wonderful seeing people so happy. The waiters arrive with the desserts, placing them before the couple, who react with oohs and aahs.

The woman reaches for her fork and gently removes a portion of the cake, bringing it towards her mouth. Her companion watches as she tastes the first morsel. Her head arches back and she lets forth a sound that's a cross between glee and something very primal.

I'll Have What She's Having

Why is it that sex and dessert are so often mentioned in the same breath?

The sounds from the couple sitting just a few feet away are positively sinful.

I flag my waiter and ask, "What is madame having?"

At this moment, the woman turns towards me and says in French, the equivalent of "it's sooo good!" followed by another sound that can only make one envious.

By now, most patrons are also interested in the scene. It's not often when you see a person enjoy a dessert so publicly and so... vocally.

That's it. My choice is made. I look at the waiter and nod towards the woman. "Bien sur, madame," he says. "Oh, and another coupe of champagne, s'il vous plaît."

Is it my imagination, or is the sun getting hotter?

The couple strolls out hand in hand, leaving us to contemplate the carnal pleasures of life.

Oh yes, food and sex. Both are essential to life, and both concern us in the most basic ways.

The first sight of a beautiful dessert revs up all our senses. I wait for my dessert with desire and anticipation. Will it meet expectations? My mouth is watering.

The waiter places the dessert before me with a flourish. A cheesecake drenched in thick crimson blackcurrant coulis and crowned with petite wild blueberries. It glistens seductively in the sunlight.

The waiter gives me a knowing look before leaving. I take my fork and gently, delicately push into the

creamy cake. It's firm and rich, but gives easily, promising tongue-tingling delights that lie ahead. As my fork pulls away a generous portion, I pause for just a moment and take one last look. I can't wait anymore. Will it be a moment of pleasure or disappointment?

Finally, the first bite. The creamy texture coats my tongue. Something is building. I can feel it. Then it happens. I am not sure whether the creamy filling is getting my attention, or the dripping blackcurrant sauce bursting with tiny wild blueberries, or the sweet, nutty almond date crust, but it's magnificent.

With a deep sigh, I let my shoulders relax. Eating dessert. The only thing more pleasurable would be eating it in the arms of a lover. Aren't the best encounters short and sweet?

When attention to the details is at its best, food is more than sensual. It is primal. It's not only seductive, but profound. It connects us, it nourishes, it provides true pleasure and helps create unforgettable memories. Food, family and friends. Healthy, happy and yours to imagine. Life is always better with dessert.

Now that's Flavour with Benefits.

Recipes + Flavours Inspired

BY PROVENCE

Everything in Provence is delicious. You will want to eat your passport just to linger a little longer! I have created several recipes inspired by the produce, sights and people of this great region.

GRILLED COFFEE-RUB RIBEYE STEAK

This one is for steak and coffee lovers. Grilled steak is a French favourite and I've decided to shake it up a bit with other favourite veggies. Capitalising on the great taste of dark roast coffee, add your favourite spices and herbs and you have a party in your mouth. Although we are using ribeye – a very high-quality cut – you can substitute any other cut you like. Grilling in a cast-iron pan gives this meat a beautiful flavour. Great for summertime feasts.

Yield: 4 servings, 14 oz (400 g)
Total Time: 45 minutes
Equipment: Cast-iron pan, BBQ grill, tongs

FLAVOURS: Grilled steak with the aromatic taste of dark coffee along with spicy hot chilli pepper and smoked paprika. The slight sweetness of the brown sugar tantalises all your taste buds.

BENEFITS: Fun and quick to make if you have a load of hungry people in your backyard needing to be fed. Steak is high in vitamin B6 and B12.

2 tbsp (16 g) ancho chile pepper

4–5 tbsp (32 g) finely ground coffee beans

4 tsp (18 g) brown sugar or (¼ tsp monk fruit)

4 tsp (9 g) smoked paprika

2½ tsp dried oregano

1½ tsp ground black pepper

2 tsp ground coriander

¾ tsp crushed red pepper flakes or ground chipotle pepper

2 tsp ground ginger

½ tsp ground sage

1 tsp turmeric

½ tsp ground cumin

1 tbsp (10 g) garlic powder

2 tsp sea salt

½ cup (125 ml) brewed coffee

2 ribeye steaks (400 g), (cut 1 inch or 2½ cm thick)

Grill temperature should be 500°F (260°C).

Put the cast-iron pan on the grill for 10 minutes before you start cooking. Place all the ingredients in a bowl (except the brewed coffee and steaks) and mix with a whisk to make the coffee rub mixture.

Put the steaks in a large bowl with the brewed coffee and make sure the entire steak is moistened with the coffee. Marinate for 5–10 minutes. Take the first steak and pat the coffee rub mixture all over both sides of the steak. Be generous. Set aside and do the same for the second steak.

Check the temperature of the cast-iron pan by dropping a few drops of water to see if droplets sizzle and dance. Gently place both steaks into the cast-iron pan using tongs, making sure the coffee rub stays on the meat.

If your cast-iron pan is small, cook one steak at a time. For medium-rare, cook the steaks 3½ minutes on each side. Cook longer if you like them well-done. Use thick oven gloves to handle the cast-iron pan as it is very hot. Remove the pan from the grill and set the meat aside to rest for 2–3 minutes.

Serve with Steamed Asparagus with "Cheese" Sauce (page 132) and Sautéed Zoodles with Sweet Pepper Purée (page 133). Use the pan gravy to pour over the steaks for extra flavour.

NUTRITION: *(per serving)*
3½ oz (100 g)

Calories	309
Fat	19.6 g
Saturated Fat	8.5 g
Cholesterol	78 mg
Carbohydrate	8.5 g
Fibre	1.8 g
Protein	26.1 g
Sugar	4.5 g
Sodium	999 mg

STEAMED ASPARAGUS WITH "CHEESE" SAUCE

Ripe asparagus steamed to perfection and then topped with a vegetable-based cheese sauce. Your guests will enjoy the cheesy flavours and textures of this side dish. They will thank you, too, because this version of a traditional favourite is cholesterol-free and very low in saturated fats. Easy, fast and healthy!

FLAVOURS: The steamed asparagus is complemented by a cheese sauce that is somewhere between a Monterey Jack and a newer cheddar cheese flavour. It is very creamy in texture from the addition of a secret ingredient – mashed potatoes.

BENEFITS: Asparagus, with its high levels of potassium and chromium, enhance the body's ability to transport insulin to manage glucose levels. Nondairy cheese also makes this a low-calorie alternative to traditional cheese sauce. The anti-inflammatory properties of turmeric, along with lots of B vitamins and minerals, make this a winner.

Yield: 4 servings
Total Time: 35 minutes
Equipment: Medium pot with a steamer pot insert

24 medium asparagus spears (384 g)

1½ cups + 1 tbsp (380 g) "cheese" sauce (see page 206), heated

Add 2 cups of water to the pot and bring to a boil, then turn down to medium-high and put the asparagus into the steamer pot. Cover and cook for 5–6 minutes.

Do not overcook or the asparagus will lose colour and nutrition. If your vegetables are done before the rest of the meal, you can plunge the asparagus into ice water while you get the rest of the meal ready. Microwave for 10 seconds to rewarm them.

Pour "cheese" sauce over vegetables to serve.

NUTRITION: *(per serving)*
6 asparagus spears with 3¼ oz (95 g) "cheese" sauce

Calories	118
Fat	5.6 g
Saturated Fat	1.1 g
Cholesterol	0 mg
Carbohydrate	16.4 g
Fibre	4.2 g
Protein	6 g
Sugar	3.5 g
Sodium	71 mg

SAUTÉED ZOODLES WITH SWEET PEPPER PURÉE

Courgette (French for zucchini) zoodles are just plain fun with their unique shape and texture. They cook really quickly, making this a great go-to side dish. With all the exposed surface area, they soak up the sauce beautifully. Put the family to work with a spiraliser to make the zoodles.

FLAVOURS: No matter what language you use to say zucchini, the mild taste is complemented by the smoky and sweet flavour of the sweet pepper purée.

BENEFITS: Affordable, fun and easy to make, these lovely zoodles are loaded with trace minerals and vitamins A, B and K. They also have high water content for your daily hydration needs.

Yield: 4 servings
Total Time: 30 minutes
Equipment: Pizza stone, cast-iron pan, a spiraliser

SWEET PEPPER PURÉE

6 mini (170 g) sweet peppers, all colours

ZOODLES

2 large zucchinis (490 g), washed, ends trimmed

½ cup (26 g) chopped onions

2 cloves garlic, pressed

2 tbsp (30 ml) filtered water

1 tsp tamari

NUTRITION: *(per serving)*
6 ½ oz (180 g)

Calories	92
Fat	0.8 g
Saturated Fat	0.1 g
Cholesterol	0 mg
Carbohydrate	20.8 g
Fibre	4.5 g
Protein	4.2 g
Sugar	12.5 g
Sodium	106 mg

SWEET PEPPER PURÉE

Preheat oven to 400°F (204°C).

Roast peppers on a hot grill or pizza stone for 5-10 minutes until slightly charred and steaming.

If you don't like the seeds, then cut the peppers open and take the seeds out. Otherwise, just remove the tops with stems and put the peppers into the food processor on high for about 45 seconds.

Set aside.

ZOODLES

Put the trimmed ends of the zucchini into the spikes of the spiraliser and turn the handle. If the zoodles are too long, you can cut them prior to cooking.

Heat the cast-iron pan over medium-high heat until drops of water sizzle. Put the onions and garlic into the pan and add the water. Sauté for about 2–3 minutes until brown and caramelised.

Add the tamari and the zoodles. Gently mix the ingredients together, being careful not to bruise the zoodles. Cook for 1–2 minutes. Add the sweet pepper purée and gently mix and cook for another 5 minutes. Test for tenderness. Do not overcook. The vegetables should still be crunchy.

Serve hot with Grilled Coffee Rub Ribeye Steak (page 130) and Steamed Asparagus with Cheese Sauce (page 132).

LAVENDER BLUEBERRY DRESSING FOR A SUMMER SALAD

You may find this surprising, but France is the world's sixth-biggest producer of blueberries. In this dish, I salute blueberries and French lavender. Fast to prepare and even faster to eat! Guests will not be able to get enough. This dressing will help salad-wary eaters love veggies and fruit. The dressing is shown here with greens, blackberries, blueberries, strawberries, black sesame seeds and pumpkin seeds.

FLAVOURS: Combining aromatic culinary lavender and tart blueberries, this dressing is sweetened with some maple extract. It's mighty addictive and can be used with fruit or vegetable salads.

BENEFITS: The chickpeas in this dressing give it protein, B vitamins, magnesium, iron, potassium and fibre. Maple extract instead of maple syrup lowers sugar and calories.

Yield: 8 oz (250 ml) 6 servings
Total Time: 15 minutes
Equipment: Food processor

½ cup (100 g) chickpeas, unsalted, drained

⅓ cup (75 ml) filtered water

½ tsp dried culinary lavender pods

1 tbsp (15 g) almond butter

1 tbsp (13 ml) maple extract

⅓ cup (50 g) wild blueberries

1–2 tbsp (14–28 ml) balsamic vinegar

Mix all of the ingredients in a food processor until smooth.

Add water slowly to achieve desired consistency. Taste along the way to ensure you are getting the flavours you want. Adjust vinegar depending on the tang level desired.

Serve over your choice of salad.

Thank you to Mary Miller for the inspiration for this recipe.

NUTRITION: *(per serving)*
3 tbsp (42 ml)

Calories	90
Fat	2.6 g
Saturated Fat	0.2 g
Cholesterol	0 mg
Carbohydrate	12.5 g
Fibre	3.4 g
Protein	3.9 g
Sugar	3 g
Sodium	5 mg

GRATIN DAUPHINOIS (POTATOES AU GRATIN)

This comfort food from southeastern France is a must for all seasons. The potatoes are baked until tender in this creamy, cheesy sauce. Entirely plant-based, it's great as a main meal or a side dish. Everyone loves this one.

Yield: 6 servings
Total Time: 1 hour
Equipment: Sharp knife, medium saucepan, mandoline or slicing attachment for food processor, mixing bowl, 2-quart (2-litre) casserole dish

5 russet potatoes (1 kg/ 2.2 lb), washed, unpeeled, sliced thinly

2 cups (506 ml) nondairy unsweetened milk

½ cup (68 ml) no added sodium vegetable broth

¾ cup (115 g) yellow onion

½ cup (30 g) nutritional yeast

½ carrot (25 g), sliced

1⅛ medium celery stalk (10 g), sliced

2 tsp onion powder

2 tsp garlic powder

½ tsp dried thyme

½ tsp turmeric powder

½ tsp smoked paprika

3 tbsp (8 g) arrowroot starch or cornstarch (22 g)

¼ cup (59 ml) cold water

pinch of salt or tamari to taste

½ cup (28 g) dried chives

¼ cup (23g) "Parmesan Cheese" (see page 212)

FLAVOURS: The cheesy and creamy texture of this dish gives potatoes a traditional familiarity.

BENEFITS: A low-calorie treat that is ready in an hour. It's filled with good carbohydrates, potassium, B vitamins, beta carotene and fibre.

Preheat oven to 425°F (218°C).

Slice the potatoes with a mandoline or food processor attachment. Put the potatoes into cold water so they do not change colour.

Add nondairy unsweetened milk, vegetable broth, onion, nutritional yeast, carrot and celery into the food processor. Process on high for 30–60 seconds until smooth.

Set the stove to medium heat and put the mixture from the food processor in a medium saucepan. Add the onion powder, garlic powder, thyme, turmeric and smoked paprika. Stir until fully incorporated. Cook for 3–4 minutes. Lower heat to allow the mixture to simmer. Stir the sauce frequently.

In a separate bowl, mix the cold water and the arrowroot starch or cornstarch until it is dissolved. Pour into the sauce mixture and stir for 5–6 minutes until the mixture thickens. Add salt or tamari to taste.

Layer one half of the potatoes on the bottom of the casserole dish. Pour half of the cheese mixture and cover all of the potatoes. Put the second layer of potatoes in the pan and pour the rest of the sauce on top, making sure all the potatoes are covered with the sauce. Top with "Parmesan Cheese". Cover the casserole dish with foil and bake for 20 minutes. Remove foil and bake for another 20 minutes. For a crispier top, broil an additional 1–2 minutes. Generously sprinkle with chives and extra "Parmesan Cheese".

NUTRITION: *(per serving)*
10½ oz (300 g)

Calories	385
Fat	16.8 g
Saturated Fat	1.4 g
Cholesterol	0 mg
Carbohydrate	48.3 g
Fibre	4.5 g
Protein	12.4 g
Sugar	4.9 g
Sodium	58 mg

GÂTEAU D'ARLES (LEMON CAKE)

This fluffy cake is a tribute to Arles and its seasonal fruits. It is vegan and oil-free, with an option to make it sugar-free. No cheating necessary here. Decorate with lemon zest and the fruits you have on hand. It will be different every time you bake it. Who says healthy can't taste great?

Yield: Two mini cakes, 3" x 7" (8 x 18 cm), 4 servings
Total Time: 50 minutes
Equipment: Two 3" x 7" (8 x 18 cm) paper or foil cake pans, cookie sheet, whisk, mixing bowls, wooden skewer, spatula, saucepan

FLAVOURS: Lemony flavour and aroma is complemented by the fluffy texture, that may surprise you. Topped with lemon glaze and seasonal fruits, it is naturally sweet and different in taste with every bite.

BENEFITS: With zero cholesterol and no added sugar, this cake is high in protein, vitamin C, fibre and trace mineral manganese. Using monk fruit lowers calories making this a cake that can be enjoyed often. Substituting tofu for eggs provides a calcium boost too.

CAKE

1 cup (125 g) unbleached cake flour

1 cup (100 g) almond flour

2 tsp baking powder

2 tsp monk fruit
or ½ cup (100 g) sugar

4½ tbsp (75 g) unsweetened applesauce

3½ tbsp almond butter

⅓ cup silken tofu (75 g)

4 tsp pure lemon extract

½ cup (122 g) nondairy milk

LEMON GLAZE

½ cup (125 ml) lemon juice

1 tsp monk fruit or
½ cup sugar 100 g

2 tsp arrowroot starch

CAKE

Preheat oven to 350°F (177°C).

In a medium bowl, whisk together the cake flour, almond flour, monk fruit (or sugar) and baking powder until well mixed. Set aside.

In a medium bowl, mix the almond butter with the applesauce until well mixed, then add the tofu and lemon extract and whisk the mixture until there are no lumps. The consistency should be such that it will pour easily into the pans.

Add the dry ingredients into the wet mixture and then half of the milk. Stir until partially mixed, and then add the other half of the milk. Mix until well blended. Divide the batter in half and place into the 2 mini cake pans. Bake for 30–32 minutes or until a wooden skewer comes out clean. Let cool for 10 minutes and remove from pans with a dull knife.

LEMON GLAZE

Toward the end of the baking time, put all the glaze ingredients into the saucepan and cook for 5–7 minutes until thickened. Add 1 more teaspoon of arrowroot starch, if you prefer a thicker glaze.

Remove the cakes from the pans while still slightly warm and pour the glaze over them and decorate with seasonal fruits and lemon zest as desired.

NUTRITION: *(per serving)*
½ cake, 4¼ oz (122 g)
monk fruit | sugar

Calories	286 | 473
Fat	12.5 g
Saturated Fat	1.2 g
Cholesterol	0 mg
Carbohydrate	33.2 g | 83 g
Fibre	3.8 g
Protein	9.3 g
Sugar	4.2 g | 54.2 g
Sodium	38 mg

TRIBUTE TO VINCENT VAN GOGH: *THE STARRY NIGHT* MAPLE BLUEBERRY DEEP-DISH PIE

This pie uses ripe wild blueberries that are cooked to perfection. The maple syrup adds another dimension to the naturally sweet flavours, and the buttery crust shatters when your fork digs in for a bite —a perfect texture that only pure, high-fat butter can bring to the party.

FLAVOURS: Sweet blueberries with a hint of maple syrup leave you wanting more.

BENEFITS: Blueberries are high in antioxidants called anthocyanin, making them a great choice for everyday snacks and this tribute pie. The pie crust is definitely not a health food, but it's great as an occasional treat.

Yield: One 9" (23 cm) pie, 8 servings
Total Time: 2–3 hours
Equipment: Food processor, glass deep-dish pie pan, saucepan, mixing bowls, wooden spoon, sharp knife, rolling pin, fork

BLUEBERRY MAPLE FILLING

5 cups (500 g) ripe wild blueberries

½–1 cup (160–320 ml) maple syrup or honey

BUTTERY PIE CRUST

2½ cups (591 g) all-purpose flour, sifted

½ tsp salt

1 package high-fat European unsalted butter (250 g), cut into cubes and frozen

6–8 tbsp (89–118 ml) ice-cold water

1 tbsp (13 g) sugar

BLUEBERRY MAPLE FILLING

To make the filling, add the blueberries and maple syrup to a saucepan and cook for 30–45 minutes on medium to low heat with the lid off. Watch carefully. You want the mixture to look like jam, not a reduction. This will prevent the pie filling from shrinking while baking and reduce the baking time.

Taste for preferred sweetness. Set aside until the pie crust and decorations are baked.

BUTTERY PIE CRUST

↪ ***If using a food processor,*** add the flour, salt and sugar. Pulse 2–3 times until combined.

Lift the lid and place the cubes of butter as evenly as possible in the food processor. Pulse 8–10 times and check the consistency. Add water a tablespoon at a time and pulse 1–2 times.

The dough should be starting to take shape. Pulse a few more times if needed, but do not overdo it. Remove the dough from the food processor and do the final shape by hand. Use a baker's scale to evenly split it. Lightly flatten the two rounds and cover in plastic wrap. Put into the refrigerator for 1 hour to chill.

↪ ***If mixing by hand,*** whisk the flour, salt and sugar in a medium mixing bowl. Cut in the frozen butter cubes a few at a time. Use a pastry cutter to mix and cut the butter until the mixture looks like small peas. Add a few drops of ice-cold water as needed to aid in mixing. Keep adding small amounts of water until the dough is cohesive and sticks together.

Shape the dough into a ball and divide in two. Use a baker's scale to evenly split it. Lightly flatten the two rounds and cover in plastic wrap. Put into the refrigerator to chill for 1 hour.

↪ ***Remove dough from refrigerator*** and roll one ball of dough onto a lightly floured surface using a floured rolling pin. Using the pie plate as a guide, or a mat with measurements on it, roll the dough to about

12 inches (30.5 cm). Fold into fourths and place carefully onto the top of the pie pan. Unfold and carefully press into the pie plate. Try not to press too hard which will make the dough uneven. Alternatively, roll the dough around the rolling pin and unroll over the pie pan.

Use a fork or your hands to make a design around the edge of the pie crust. Take a fork and press the tines into the bottom of the pie crust to make a series of holes. This will help the bottom crust bake properly and keep it from doming.

Put the pie pan into the freezer and freeze for 1 hour. This will help the crust bake properly. When ready to bake, remove the pan from the freezer.

Pour the cooked pie filling into the pie pan. For better browning of the outer crust, brush with milk and sprinkle with sugar. Bake on the bottom rack of the oven for 30–45 minutes until the crust is deep brown. You can use a pie crust protector to keep the outer crust from over-browning. If the pie filling is drying out during the bake, it can be lightly covered with foil for the balance of the cooking time. Set aside to cool.

PIE CRUST DECORATIONS
- Sanding sugars – yellow, white and blue
- Wilton or other edible dyes
- Fine food-grade paint brushes
- Second round of pie crust rolled out
- Cookie cutters
- Sharp knife
- Cookie sheet
- Parchment paper

Ornaments can be baked after the pie is done since the pie cannot be decorated hot. The sugar will sink in and disappear.

Decide what design you are going to use and cut out the necessary shapes with cookie cutters and a sharp knife.

Use edible dyes and sanding sugars to decorate the pie ornaments.

Put ornaments onto parchment paper and bake for 8–10 minutes at 375°F (191°C). Watch carefully so you do not burn them. Make extras in case of accidents.

After the pie is well cooled, set decorations onto the pie very carefully so they do not sink in. Decorate the rest of the pie with sanding sugars.

Serve immediately.

Thank you to Tara Jensen, author of *A Baker's Year: Twelve Months of Baking and Living the Simple Life at the Smoke Signals Bakery* for the cooking tips on blueberry filling and making pie crust by hand.

NUTRITION: *(per serving)*
1 slice, 7¼ oz (205 g)

Calories	307
Fat	10.2 g
Saturated Fat	6.3 g
Cholesterol	27 mg
Carbohydrate	49.3 g
Fibre	1.1 g
Protein	4 g
Sugar	18.1 g
Sodium	150 mg

LEMON LAVENDER LUXURY CHEESECAKE

This luxurious cake celebrates the famous yellow colour of the region. Flavourful and gluten-free for those who are celiac, it has an easy faux-lemon curd, complimented by lavender. The subtle flavours will take you to Provence no matter where you are. Decorate with a floral topping and lemon rinds to complete the summer-in-Provence mood. It's so easy, anyone can make this cheesecake!

FLAVOURS: It cannot get more Provençal than lavender. The subtle flavours of the lavender and lemon are refreshing in this creamy filling. The subtle sweetness of the almond crust makes this one an exciting blend of flavours.

BENEFITS: Gluten-free for those with allergies. The almond crust is loaded with vitamin E. The filling is high in calcium and is lower in calories than traditional cheesecakes.

Yield: One 9-inch (23 cm) cheesecake, serves 8
Total Time: 3 hours
Equipment: 9-inch (23 cm) springform pan, greased cookie sheet, parchment paper, food processor or hand mixer, small and medium mixing bowls, plastic wrap, spatulas, zester, mortar and pestle

CRUST

2 cups (192 g) almond flour

8 tbsp (113 g) unsalted butter

CHEESECAKE FILLING

1 can (300 ml) condensed milk

½ cup (125 ml) lemon juice, fresh squeezed

1 tsp culinary lavender

3 eggs

12½ oz (350 g) Icelandic-style (Skyr) plain yoghurt, room temperature

11½ oz (325 g), plain cream cheese, room temperature

pinch of salt

1 tsp vanilla extract

1 lemon peeled in strips and 2 lemons zested for decoration

culinary lavender, to decorate

CRUST

Preheat oven to 375°F (191°C).

Place ingredients in a mixing bowl and combine using your hands or a large spoon. Place parchment paper into the springform pan. Press the crust evenly into the bottom of the pan. If it is too sticky, use a piece of plastic wrap over the mixture and continue to press into the crust mixture until even. Remove plastic wrap from pan.

Bake for 12–15 minutes or until golden brown and crust is pulling away from the sides. Remove from the oven and set aside. While the crust is baking, prepare the filling.

CHEESECAKE FILLING

Lower temperature to 350°F (177°C).

Mix condensed milk and lemon juice in a small bowl until the juice has slightly curdled the condensed milk. Set aside.

Use a mortar and pestle to crush the lavender pods until you can smell the aroma. Add lavender, condensed milk mixture, eggs, yoghurt, cream cheese, salt and vanilla to the food processor and mix thoroughly on medium speed. Blend until smooth for about 1 minute. Make sure it is completely blended. Scrape sides of food processor as needed. Pour ingredients into baked crust.

Bake for 30 minutes. When the cheesecake is done, it will move a little in the centre but should still have a done look, not so jiggly. If it is still wet in the centre, bake for 5–10 minutes more. The edges of the cake should pull away from the sides of the pan slightly. Do not overbake.

Cool at room temperature for about an hour to cause less cracking on the top. Let cool in the refrigerator for at least 2 hours or preferably overnight.

Gently release the cake from the springform pan using a dull knife around the inside edge. Open the spring and carefully remove the cake. If it cracks a little, decorate the top and cover any broken areas.

Decorate the entire cake with shaved lemon rind, lemon zest and lavender. Add whipped cream or frosting for additional garnishes.

NUTRITION: *(per serving)*
1 slice, 6¾ oz (195 g)

Calories	473
Fat	34.2 g
Saturated Fat	18.8 g
Cholesterol	148 mg
Carbohydrate	24.1 g
Fibre	0.8 g
Protein	13.4 g
Sugar	22.3 g
Sodium	303 mg

CHERRY CLAFOUTIS

This traditional French version is usually made with unpitted cherries, but that made me a bit nervous. This version has a decorative look with the cherries, pitted sides up. I like making it in a cast-iron pan as it bakes evenly and makes for a lovely presentation. If your pan is well seasoned, the cake comes out easily. You can lower the calories if you choose monk fruit instead of sugar.

FLAVOURS: The sweet cherries come through, both sweet and tart, supported by the eggy textures. Almond flour brings a nutty sweetness to the palate.

BENEFITS: This is a light, easy breakfast cake, and it works for those with gluten and dairy allergies. High levels of vitamin E, along with cholesterol-lowering oat flour, make this one great for breakfast.

Yield: One 10-inch (25 cm) cake, 6 servings
Total Time: 1 hour 45 minutes
Equipment: Food processor, 10-inch (25 cm) cast-iron pan

1½ cups (250 g) red or yellow cherries, pitted

1 tsp arrowroot starch

3 eggs

1 cup (245 g) unsweetened nondairy yoghurt (i.e. coconut yoghurt)

⅓ cup (32 g) almond flour

½ cup (35 g) oat flour or other gluten-free flour

2 tbsp (28 g) nondairy butter, melted or 1 tbsp canola oil

⅓ cup sugar (66 g) or ½ tsp monk fruit

spray oil for pan

Decorating Sugar Revisited (see page 208)

Make sure pitted cherries are dry and toss with arrowroot starch. Put them into the freezer in a medium-sized bowl for about 30 minutes.

Preheat oven to 400°F (204°C).

Put the eggs, yoghurt, almond flour, oat flour, melted nondairy butter and sugar (or monk fruit) into a food processor. Purée until smooth. Scrape sides to make sure it all is incorporated. Set aside for about 30 minutes.

Spray the cast-iron pan or pie pan with oil. Pour egg mixture into the prepared pan. Carefully place each cherry with the cut side up and pack the egg mixture with as many cherries as possible, so there is very little egg mixture visible. Be careful not to press the cherries down too much, because you want them to be visible on top of the finished product.

Bake in the middle rack of the oven for 30–35 minutes or until golden brown. Let cool for 5–10 minutes. Dust with Decorating Sugar Revisited or powdered sugar if desired. Decorate with a few whole cherries.

NUTRITION: *(per serving)*
1 slice, 4½ oz (125 g)

	monk fruit	sugar
Calories	240	282
Fat	17 g	
Saturated Fat	10.2 g	
Cholesterol	92 mg	
Carbohydrate	17.9 g	28.9 g
Fibre	2.9 g	
Protein	6.9 g	
Sugar	6.1 g	17.1 g
Sodium	42 mg	

RHUBARB TART

France may not be well known for rhubarb, but it does grow there. Everything that's delicious grows there! This tart is dedicated to Arles, where so much art and literature was inspired by the incredible sights, aromas and flavours of the region. It is baked using a special French tart pan, which is ingenious with a lift-out pan bottom. You never touch or damage the crust. It is vegan and dairy-free, and yet the crust is light and moist.

Yield: 9" (23 cm) tart, 9 servings
Total Time: 1 hour
Equipment: 9" (23 cm) tart pan with removable bottom, saucepan, sharp knife, large mixing bowl, rolling pin, pastry brush, small mixing bowls

FLAVOURS: This dessert is all rhubarb, with the tart flavour offset by a hint of raspberry to colour the filling and sweeten it naturally. The almond crust gives it a nice texture and nuttiness.

BENEFITS: Low in calories and saturated fats – and cholesterol-free – this dessert may become one of your go-to party recipes. It's fast to make and beautiful, no matter what you do with the top. Rich in vitamin K and calcium, it is fun and nutritious. By substituting sugar with pure monk fruit, you can reduce your calories by 30% and sugar by 85%.

CRUST

1½ cups (170 g) fine almond flour

½ cup (70 g) brown rice flour

½ cup (60 g) tapioca flour

¼ tsp sea salt

½ tsp monk fruit or 2 tbsp (25 g) sugar

½ tsp almond extract

8 tbsp (118 ml) cold water

FILLING

2½ cups (300 g) or 4–6 medium stalks rhubarb, sliced

4 tbsp (38 g) instant tapioca

2 tsp pectin

1 cup + 3 tbsp (280 ml) water

½ tsp monk fruit or ½ cup (100 g) sugar

¾ cup (50 g) raspberries

CRUST

Preheat oven to 350°F (177°C).

In a large mixing bowl, whisk together the dry ingredients. In a separate bowl, mix the almond extract with 6 tablespoons of water. (Reserve 2 tablespoons of water for use only if the crust mixture is too dry.)

Add the almond extract water mixture to the dry ingredients and mix with your hands until it feels moist. If it is too crumbly, add the remaining 2 tablespoons of water 1 at a time, as needed. Form into a ball.

Put parchment paper down on the counter and place the dough on top. Roll out the dough into a flat disk shape.

Place the dough into the tart pan and press the dough to fit all across the bottom and up the sides. Use a sharp knife to cut the top of the dough off evenly if any of it is above the tart pan edge. You want a smooth edge as this will be exactly how it looks when it is baked.

Use the tines of a fork to puncture the bottom to allow air to escape and prevent doming.

You can place the pie tin directly into the oven or onto a cookie sheet to make it easier to retrieve without disturbing the crust or, later, the filling.

Bake for 15 minutes until light brown. It will bake some more with the filling, so do not overbake.

FILLING

While the tart crust is baking, place all filling ingredients into a saucepan and cook over medium heat. Stir often for about 10–15 minutes until the mixture becomes thick and the rhubarb has fallen apart. Set aside and allow to cool. The finished weight of the filling should be 540 g or approximately 2¾ cups.

TO FINISH THE TOP

6–8 stalks (400–600 g) rhubarb as even in width as possible

¼ cup (57 g) caster sugar or ¼ tsp monk fruit

¼ cup (59 ml) filtered water

Mix the caster sugar or monk fruit with water.

Cut desired shapes and sizes. Trimming may be required. Use a pastry brush or your fingers to brush the top of each piece of rhubarb with the sugar/water mixture. This will ensure they do not dry out in the oven.

ASSEMBLY

Pour the filling into the baked tart shell and evenly distribute it along the bottom. It should come halfway up the tart shell.

Place the rhubarb pieces carefully on top of the filling. Do not press or they may sink. Carefully arrange them as it is difficult to pull them out and rearrange them. The pieces are going to move slightly when laid onto the tart filling.

Bake for 15–20 minutes or until the rhubarb looks cooked and the top of the crust is golden brown. Remove and cool on wire rack. Cut when cool.

Thank you to Lori Rasmussen at @myquietkitchen for inspiration on the tart crust.

NUTRITION: *(per serving)*
1 slice, 4 oz (115 g)
monk fruit | sugar

Calories	185 | 260
Fat	4.4 g
Saturated Fat	0.4 g
Cholesterol	0 mg
Carbohydrate	20.8 g | 40.8 g
Fibre	3.8 g
Protein	3 g
Sugar	1.7 g | 21.7 g
Sodium	59 mg

The coastline of the Calanques is spectacular

Marseille

MIRROR ON THE MEDITERRANEAN

Marseille

AND THE CALANQUES

Marseille, the capital of Provence, is the oldest and second-largest city in France. Situated on the Mediterranean, it was founded by the Greeks around 600 BC as a trading port. It has a diverse population of roughly one million and a spirit and style all its own. During the French Revolution, 500 volunteers from Marseille marched to Paris singing what would later become the French national anthem, "La Marseillaise". In World War II, the city was an active centre of the French resistance. The city has eight mayors who run the 16 arrondissements (districts).

It has a completely different feel than the rest of France with its warm climate and connection to the sea. I first fell in love with Marseille when my parents rented an apartment there for a vacation during our year in France. They loved taking us for evening strolls around the boardwalk that surrounds the Vieux (Old) Port. It is charming and ever-changing with hundreds of masts bobbing up and down courtesy of the many boats moored at the marina.

Take time to visit areas such as *Le Panier* to discover the feel of "old" Marseille. Explore some of the extensive parks of Château du Pharo, Château Borély, and Palais Longchamp. Enjoy the panoramic view from the city's best-known symbol, Basilique Notre-Dame de la Garde (Our Lady of the Guard), overlooking the city.

Or, take a boat tour and visit the Île d'If and its château, one of the memorable settings in Alexandre Dumas' adventure novel *The Count of Monte Cristo*. The other alternative is to take a seat at one of the cafés and watch the world stroll by.

Hundreds of yachts and sailboats moored in Marseille's Vieux (Old) Port

Go for a walk early in the morning to get the best selection of fresh fish at one of the Old Port's fish stalls

Influences from Italy and North Africa help to create food and culture that is dynamic, just like its current inhabitants. The cuisine of Marseille is heavily influenced by the sea, as shown by its famous *bouillabaisse* (fish soup), found everywhere.

Speaking of the sea, I had an incredible dinner at L'Épuisette – a one-star Michelin restaurant run by Chef Guillaume Sourrieu. The artistic presentation of the lobster medallion with celery remoulade, dotted with hazelnuts, was first class. I loved the decadent Tonka bean chocolate cake topped with vanilla and served with house-made orange sorbet. Seated by a picture window, my meal was matched only by the view of the water crashing on the rock outcroppings, set against a spectacular sunset.

Basilique Notre-Dame de la Garde provides the best views of Marseille

The port of Vallons (small valley) des Auffes in the 7th arrondissement of Marseille

The entrance into the Old Port of Marseille (Fort St. Jean centre) with a view from the Aix-Marseille University

Men gossiping in the early morning in a restaurant open 24/7 near the Old Port

Julia Child in Marseille (MC660-1-28) taken by her husband, Paul Child
Credit: Photograph by Paul Child. © Schlesinger Library, Radcliffe Institute, Harvard University

Inspired by Julia

> "The best way to execute French cooking is to get good and loaded and whack the hell out of a chicken."
>
> Julia Child

Did you know that Julia Child lived in France, including Marseille, while she was researching, creating and painstakingly documenting French recipes? She began cooking and experimenting with food in her 30s when her husband's work took them to post-war France in 1948.

Her work would be introduced to the American public in 1961 when the brilliant editor, Judith Jones of Knopf Publishing, rescued it from the rejection pile. For over a decade, Julia had slaved over the 726-page cookbook, *Mastering the Art of French Cooking*, with co-authors Simone Beck and Louisette Bertholle. They were dear friends and cooks with whom she founded a home-based cooking school in Paris, *L'École des Trois Gourmandes*. The book was for American home cooks who wanted to learn the basics of French cuisine.

But Julia's first recipe was apparently "shark repellent", created as a solution to keep sharks away from anti-submarine mines during World War II. This is fact, not fiction. During the war, she worked for the Office of Strategic Services (OSS), which later became the CIA. While she was working for the OSS in China, she met her future husband, Paul Child, who took the picture on the facing page.

My mother loved watching Julia Child's *The French Chef* on the Public Broadcasting System (PBS) in the United States. Her TV shows incorporated the use of many fresh ingredients, and the grocery industry noticed an uptick in demand for the same ingredients used on the program. My mother was a foreign language teacher and would play episodes of *The French Chef* to her students to help inspire their learning of the French language. Julia's forthright manner and humour made everyone laugh.

Julia was so enamoured with France and was such an ambassador for French cuisine in the United States that the French Government awarded her the *Légion d'Honneur* (Legion of Honour) in 2000, France's highest honour. She died in 2004 at 91. Her last meal was a bowl of French onion soup.

Drift Along

THE MEDITERRANEAN COAST

East of Marseille, near the delightful town of Cassis, is the Parc National des Calanques. The "Parc" has many *falaises* (cliffs) and steep sheltered *calanques* (inlets). The combination of limestone and pine trees overlooking the waterways is another characteristic that makes Provence so breathtaking. Take a boat ride into one of the calanques. You will find that there is a certain magic in the light – something about the combination of the blue water, the cliffs, the people and, of course, the sun.

Once back on shore, why not savour a glass of the local Cassis wine with regional fish, and perhaps a fruit or chocolate-based dessert?

The beautiful Calanque d'En Vau just a few kilometres west of the town of Cassis

The Château de Cassis overlooking the town of Cassis

The view from Falaises de Cassis overlooking the city of Cassis

Recipes + Flavours Inspired

BY MARSEILLE & CASSIS

The eclectic mixture of ancient cultures and dramatic landscapes of this region make for an abundance of food and ingredient choices. Marseille's celebrated history, with its charming waterfront, has inspired me to create some dishes that will delight your eyes and your palate.

FRENCH ONION SOUP – A CLASSIC REVISITED

This recipe pays tribute to Julia Child and her original French onion soup. The deep rich colour of the soup comes from the beautiful onions, which have been cooked and browned. With its many ingredients, it's best to do your prep ahead of time for optimal results. I hope that it will surprise you, both with its authenticity and its differences. This dish is often served in classic tureens with croutons and cheese on top.

FLAVOURS: Deeply browned and caramelised onions, along with whisky and white wine, give this soup flavours that work from the front to the back of your mouth. The cheesy crouton will leave you wanting more. Natural sugars give it a pleasing sweetness.

BENEFITS: Calories are 40% fewer than the classic version, and it's lower in saturated fats, sodium and cholesterol. It also has fibre, calcium and natural sugars from the onions and sauce additions. This healthy version is a winner in every way.

Yield: 4 tureens of soup
Total Time: 2 hours
Equipment: Food processor, large pot, spatula, tureens

3 tbsp (45 g) "Worcestershire" sauce (see page 214)

3 large onions (680 g), peeled, thinly sliced and cut in half

6 tbsp (89 ml) filtered water

4 garlic cloves (20 g), pressed

½ cup (118 ml) dry white wine or water

2½ cups (248 ml) "Beef" broth (see page 204)

2 bay leaves

½–1 tbsp (4 g) dried thyme

½ tsp ground black pepper

1 tbsp (14 ml) brandy or whisky

4 slices baguette (124 g), cut to 1-inch (2.5 cm) thick slices

¾ cup (168 g) "Gruyère Cheese" (see page 211)

4 tbsp (64 g) "Parmesan Cheese" (see page 212)

Place a large pot over medium heat. Add the "Worcestershire" sauce and the onions to the pot and toss to coat with the sauce. Caramelise the onions by stirring constantly for 10 minutes.

Increase the heat to medium-high and add 6 tablespoons of water to the mixture. Stir often for 5–10 minutes. Make sure they do not burn.

Add pressed garlic and mix to incorporate and cook for 5–10 more minutes. The onions should have a different aroma as they brown.

Deglaze the pot with either white wine or water. Stir and release all the brown bits stuck to the bottom of the pot.

Add the "Beef" broth, bay leaves and thyme. Bring to a simmer, cover and allow to bubble slowly for 30 minutes.

Season with more salt and pepper as desired. Discard bay leaves. Add whisky or brandy, if using.

While the soup is simmering, toast the bread in the toaster until it is golden brown. Set aside.

When soup is done, ladle into oven-proof soup bowls and place the toast on top. Cover the toast with "Gruyère" and "Parmesan cheeses". Put under the broiler for 3–5 minutes or until the "cheese" is brown. Watch carefully as it will burn quickly.

Serve with slices of raw onions or a dash of paprika for colour.

NUTRITION: (per serving) 1 tureen, 12¼ oz (350 g)	
Calories	296
Fat	6.5 g
Saturated Fat	1.2 g
Cholesterol	0 mg
Carbohydrate	48.7 g
Fibre	7.5 g
Protein	12 g
Sugar	10.1 g
Sodium	527 mg

SALAD NIÇOISE - INSPIRED BY JULIA CHILD

Who knew a salad could stir up so much controversy? The "right ingredients" for Salad Niçoise can get a conversation going in France. This version will stir up a fuss because it is oil-free, vegan and has "faux eggs" as a suggested ingredient. It is also *composée* – composed or presented rather than tossed.

Yield: 4 servings
Total Time: 45 minutes
Equipment: Pot, steamer insert, sharp knife, mixing bowls

SALAD

1 cup (150 g) or 16 large green beans

8+ large romaine leaves (313 g), washed

1 cup (174 g) French Potato Salad (see page 113)

3–4 Faux oeuf dur (60–80 g) (see page 209) or regular hard-boiled eggs

3 tbsp (34 g) capers

⅓ cup (60 g) black or green olives, pitted

½ cup (100 g) cherry tomatoes, sliced

DRESSING

¼ cup (80 ml) water

3 tbsp (22 ml) lemon juice

1 tsp lemon zest

¼ cup (58 ml) white wine vinegar

2 tsp onion powder

1 tsp sea salt or tamari

½ tsp ground black pepper

FLAVOURS: There are many flavours in this dish, from the Faux oeuf dur ("faux eggs") with their Dijon mustard notes to the salty olives, green beans and crunchy capers. The fresh white wine vinegar dressing and romaine lettuce give it an earthy taste and great crunch.

BENEFITS: Compared to the traditional version, this salad has more fibre and good carbohydrates, allowing you to feel satisfied longer. This salad has zero cholesterol and almost no saturated fats. It is rich in potassium and calcium, making it a healthy and tasty alternative.

SALAD

Steam the green beans for 6–8 minutes. Put them into cold water to stop the cooking process. Set aside until needed.

Separate romaine leaves and cut or leave whole as presented. This salad is generally placed on the leaves for presentation, not tossed.

Arrange the ingredients in groups on the plate as shown in the picture or in another arrangement of your choice.

DRESSING

Add dressing ingredients to a bowl and stir until fully incorporated. Drizzle dressing on the entire salad or allow guests to pour their own dressing.

Use fresh ground pepper as desired.

NUTRITION: *(per serving)*
8¾ oz (250 g)

Calories	291
Fat	2.0 g
Saturated Fat	0.4 g
Cholesterol	0 mg
Carbohydrate	53.9 g
Fibre	18.7 g
Protein	16.3 g
Sugar	4.5 g
Sodium	334 mg

SEA BASS CASSIS

Sea bass is a popular fish in the Mediterranean. When it's baked correctly, it's the perfect main dish – and it's simple and fast to prepare. Pair it with fresh vegetables such as tomatoes, baked potatoes and asparagus, and you have a meal that everyone will love. As a salute to this unique region, finish this mild fish with pungent sweet Crème de Cassis, a blackcurrant liqueur from Burgundy which is available around the world.

FLAVOURS: The combination of mildly sweet fish and Crème de Cassis adds a unique flavour to this dish. The meat is soft and dense, with a satisfying texture as it meets your fork. There is no "fishy" taste for those wary of seafood.

BENEFITS: This is a high-protein fish that is loaded with B vitamins and potassium, which regulates blood pressure and prevents osteoporosis.

Yield: 4 servings
Total Time: 20 minutes
Equipment: Large pan, sharp knife

16 oz (452 g) fresh sea bass

2½ oz (77 ml) Crème de Cassis

salt and ground black pepper, to taste

Preheat the oven to 450°F (232°C).

Line a large pan with foil and place the fish on the foil. Bake for 15 minutes and check for doneness. It should start flaking. Do not overcook. If necessary, bake for 5 minutes more.

Cut into four pieces and drizzle Crème de Cassis over the fish. Add sea salt and ground pepper to taste. Serve immediately with fresh tomatoes, steamed asparagus and oven-baked sliced potatoes.

NUTRITION: *(per serving)*
4 oz (113 g)

Calories	143
Fat	2.1 g
Saturated Fat	0.5 g
Cholesterol	44mg
Carbohydrate	0 g
Fibre	0 g
Protein	19.6 g
Sugar	0 g
Sodium	72 mg

FRITES AU FOUR (BAKED FRENCH FRIES)

Potatoes are a worldwide staple and a favourite, but they are often considered to be unhealthy because of the cooking methods used, such as deep-frying. Still, they are a healthy carbohydrate loaded with minerals. This recipe rescues the reputation of the humble potato and adds some great flavours that everyone will enjoy. No peeling necessary. You can't beat that!

FLAVOURS: Depending on the variety of potato you use, these frites have a mild taste with a nice texture. I also ramp up the flavour with some spices and herbs. The cumin brings out "beefy" notes, and the paprika and red pepper flakes bring smokiness. The sweetness of the mustard paired with aromatic tarragon and marjoram finishes it off. You can also choose to dip the frites in "Worcestershire" sauce for a tangy and sweet finish.

BENEFITS: Unlike traditional French fries, these baked frites have fewer calories and saturated fats. They are also rich in fibre, have half the iron of a 3 oz (85 g) steak, and more potassium than a banana. We leave the skins on because that's where the nutrition is. Great for hungry families who crave this classic dish.

Yield: 4 servings
Total Time: 40 minutes
Equipment: Sharp knife, large roasting pan, parchment paper, sealable plastic bag or bowl with tight cover, tongs

---

3 small or 2 large red potatoes (350 g), washed (see note)

---

1 tsp garlic powder

1–2 tsp onion powder

---

1 tsp tarragon

½ tsp dried sage

---

1 tsp cumin

---

1 tsp sea salt

½ tsp red pepper flakes

½ tsp thyme

½ tsp dried mustard powder

---

1 tsp turmeric

---

1 tsp smoked paprika

---

1 tsp marjoram

½ cup (275 ml) "Worcestershire" sauce (see page 214)

Preheat oven to 425°F (224°C).

Wash the potatoes carefully and cut out any bad spots. With the skins on, cut the potatoes in half lengthwise and put the flat side down. Cut in half lengthwise again. Cut the potatoes again to get the size you want. Try to keep them the same size to get even baking. Thicker potato slices will take longer to bake. Wash the starch off the fries and dry off with a towel.

To flavour the potatoes, put the garlic powder, onion powder, tarragon, dried sage, cumin, sea salt, red pepper flakes, thyme, mustard powder, turmeric, smoked paprika and marjoram into a large plastic bag or a large bowl. Put the potatoes in the bag or the bowl and seal tightly. Shake until all the potatoes are covered in the herb mix. Put parchment paper or a barbeque cooking sheet in the bottom of a large pan. Place the potatoes in the pan, in a single layer to assure proper baking.

Bake for 15–20 minutes. The potatoes should start to show some blistering on top. Jiggle the fries with tongs and turn them over. Bake another 5–10 minutes until they are browned and blistered on both sides. Remove them from the pan and serve immediately with condiments such as "Worcestershire" sauce, mustard, ketchup or salsa. Use any extra spices left in the bag to sprinkle over the frites.

Note: When frying potatoes, many people use the russet potato. Russet potatoes are high in starch, which is why they work best when deep frying. But red potatoes are recommended for this recipe as a high level of starch is not needed for baked fries. Red potatoes are also more nutritious than russets.

NUTRITION: *(per serving)*
3 oz (85 g)
baked | fried

Calories	119 | 274
Fat	0.7 g | 14.4 g
Saturated Fat	0.1 g | 3.4 g
Cholesterol	0 mg | 0 mg
Carbohydrate	27.9 g | 31.9 g
Fibre	3.5 g | 3 g
Protein	3.6 g | 3.2 g
Sugar	2.1 g | 0.6 g
Sodium	125 mg |165 mg

CLASSIC BAGUETTE

Who doesn't love baguettes? This is a tribute to people walking down a French street with a baguette under their arm and tearing off a piece as they stroll. That is such an endearing image of French culture and life. This recipe has the technique to replicate this iconic bread.

FLAVOURS: Yeasty, crispy baguette with that classic French bread taste. Making it yourself will give your kitchen and home that comforting and familiar baked bread aroma.

BENEFITS: Devour this one for pure pleasure! Homemade bread also allows you to control the ingredients, such as salt and the type of flour used.

Yield: 3 baguettes, 4 servings per baguette
Total Time: 20 hours
Equipment: Mixing bowls, shower cap, baguette pan, baker's scale, parchment paper, bench knife, baker's peel, lame

STARTER

½ cup (113 ml) cool water

¹⁄₁₆ tsp active dry yeast or instant yeast

1 cup (120 g) all-purpose unbleached flour

DOUGH

all of the starter

1½ tsp active dry yeast or instant yeast

1 cup + 2 tablespoons (255 ml) lukewarm water

3½ cups (418 g) all purpose unbleached flour

1½ tsp high mineral salt

STARTER

Mix all ingredients together with a spoon. A soft dough should form. Cover (I use a shower cap) and let rest at room temperature for about 12–14 hours or overnight. If the room temperature is cold overnight, a good way to keep it warmer is to put it into the microwave or a cold oven. The starter should be bubbly and should have expanded.

DOUGH

Mix the starter and all the dough ingredients together by hand or with a mixer. Knead for 4–5 minutes. If using a stand mixer, knead on speed 2. The finished dough should stick to the bottom of the bowl.

Place the dough in a large mixing bowl and cover with a shower cap. Make sure the bowl is big enough so that the dough does not rise and stick to the shower cap or plastic wrap. Let rise for about 45 minutes. Gently deflate the dough and fold its edges into the centre, then turn it over in the bowl and let it rise covered for another 45 minutes. It should be noticeably puffy at this point.

Turn the dough onto a lightly floured workspace. Gently deflate. Weigh the dough and divide into 3 equal pieces with a bench knife.

Shape the dough into rough balls by pulling the edges into the centre. Cover with lightly greased plastic wrap and let rest for 15 minutes.

Take the first ball of dough and flatten the dough slightly and then fold it almost in half, sealing the edges with the heel of your hand. Turn the dough around and repeat. Fold and then flatten. Repeat this process and the dough will start to elongate.

With the seam side down, cup your fingers and gently roll the dough into a 16" (40 cm) log. The end goal is 15" (38 cm), so this allows for shrinkage. Taper each end in the typical baguette pointy style.

Repeat with the other two balls of dough.

Place the logs seam-side down onto a parchment-lined sheet pan or Italian loaf pan or pans. Alternatively, place in the folds of a heavily floured cotton dish towel (*couche*). Cover lightly with a damp towel or greased plastic wrap and allow dough to continue to rise and become puffy or "marshmallowy". The rise will be less dense, but will not be doubled in size, in about 45 minutes at 68°F (20°C).

Towards the end of the rising time, preheat the oven to 450°F (232°C) and put a pan with 1½ cups of water on the lower rack. If using a baking stone to bake the bread, put it on the middle rack.

Once your baguettes have risen, roll them seam-side down onto a parchment-lined or nonstick pan. If using a baking stone, roll them onto a piece of parchment paper and lift the parchment onto the pan or stone. A baker's peel can be used to ensure a safe move into the pan(s) or onto the stone.

Using a lame or a razor blade held at a 45-degree angle, cut or score the baguette with 3–5 diagonal slashes across the top of each loaf.

Load the baguettes into the oven. If you are using a stone, use the baker's peel to safely move the bread into the oven. The water in the pan should be boiling, so use long oven mitts to protect yourself from a steam burn while moving the bread into the oven. The steam will give them a shiny crust.

Bake the baguettes for 24–28 minutes or until they are a deep golden brown. Remove them from the oven and cool on a rack.

For crispier baguettes, turn off the oven, crack it open 2 inches (5 cm) and allow the baguettes to cool completely in the oven.

Thank you to the King Arthur Baking Company for recipe inspiration.

NUTRITION: *(per serving)*
¼ baguette, 2¾ oz (78 g)

Calories	165
Fat	0.5 g
Saturated Fat	0.1 g
Cholesterol	0 mg
Carbohydrate	34.4 g
Fibre	1.3 g
Protein	4.8 g
Sugar	0.1 g
Sodium	292 mg

Old Port Marseille

CLASSIC FRENCH COUNTRY SWEET POTATO WALNUT BREAD

When I want colour and flavour in a French country bread, I usually add sweet potatoes or *patates douces*. I also like to throw in walnuts, which are a staple in France and are used in many tarts and breads. The air bubbles in this bread make it a light and delicious accompaniment to any meal.

Yield: 2 small loaves or 1 large loaf (16 slices of bread)
Total Time: 20 hours
Equipment: Baker's scale, mixing bowls, shower cap or plastic wrap, brotforms, parchment paper, cutting board, bench knife, lame, baking stone, baker's thermometer

STARTER

1 cup (237 ml) lukewarm water 100°F (38°C)
½ tsp active dry yeast
1¼ cups (149 g) unbleached all-purpose flour
¼ cup (33 g) whole wheat flour (preferably organic)
½ tsp vital wheat gluten

DOUGH

all of the starter
1 cup (237 ml) lukewarm water 100°F (38°C)
¾ tsp active dry yeast
1 cup + 2 tbsp (255 ml) lukewarm water
¼ cup (50 g) rye flour (preferably dark rye)
3½–3¾ cups (400 to 430 g) all purpose unbleached flour
1 cup (200 g) baked mashed sweet potato
3 tbsp (20 g) walnuts, crushed
1½–2 tsp high mineral salt
¼ cup brown rice flour, to dust brotforms

FLAVOURS: The hint of sweet potato gives this airy, yeasty bread a sweet lift, and the walnuts add an unexpected nutty crunch. No empty carbohydrates here.

BENEFITS: Loaded with beta carotene, antioxidants and vitamin A, sweet potatoes are one of the most nutritious foods you can eat. Walnuts are also a great source of vitamin E and omega-3s. These additions enrich the bread and boost your gut health.

STARTER

Mix all ingredients together with a spoon to form a pudding-like mixture. Cover (I use a shower cap) and let rest at room temperature for 2–16 hours or overnight. If the room temperature is cold overnight, a good way to keep it warmer is to put it into the microwave or a cold oven. The starter should be bubbly and expanded.

DOUGH

Stir down the starter and add the water and yeast. Stir and let rest for 5 minutes to let the yeast hydrate. Add the rye and 3 cups of the all-purpose flour (390 g). Mix and let rest for 10 minutes. Stir again and add the salt. The dough will start to firm up. Add ¼ cup (60 g) more all-purpose flour, if needed. Using less flour increases the airiness of the bread. Add the sweet potatoes and walnuts. Mix all ingredients together by hand or with a mixer and knead for 10–12 minutes. The dough will start to become less sticky and more cohesive.

Place the dough in a large mixing bowl and cover with a lightly oiled shower cap or plastic wrap. If the weather is warm and humid, the rise may take 1–2 hours. If it is colder, put the dough into the microwave to keep it warm.

Take the dough out of the bowl and put it onto a floured cutting board. Deflate the dough gently. Do not knock all the air bubbles out or the bread will not be light and airy. Weigh the dough and shape into two balls or keep as one large loaf.

Flour the brotforms with rice flour and put each loaf inside. Cover with plastic wrap or a shower cap and place in the refrigerator for 1 hour to allow easier scoring of the bread.

Put a pan with 1½ cups of water onto the bottom rack and turn the oven to 475°F (246°C). Place the baking stone (if using) onto the middle rack of the oven. Heat for 45–60 minutes.

Place the baker's peel on the counter and put parchment paper on the peel. Place the peel with the parchment paper on the brotform, dough side up. Invert or rotate the peel holding the brotform until the brotform is upside down with the brotform on top and the dough side down. Gently lift the brotform off the dough. Let gravity allow the dough to come out of the brotform.

While dough is still on the baker's peel, use a lame or a razor blade, held at a 45-degree angle, and cut or score the loaf in your desired pattern. Use the baker's peel to move the loaf to the baking stone in the oven. Repeat with the second loaf.

Reduce heat to 425°F (218°C) and bake for 25–30 minutes or until golden brown. If you have a baking thermometer, internal temperature should be around 200°F (93°C).

Remove from the oven. Place on a wire rack to cool completely before slicing.

Thank you to King Arthur Baking Company for inspiration for the recipe.

NUTRITION: *(per serving)*
1 slice of small loaf,
3 oz (85 g)

Calories	127
Fat	1.2 g
Saturated Fat	0.1 g
Cholesterol	0 mg
Carbohydrate	25.1 g
Fibre	1.8 g
Protein	3.9 g
Sugar	0.9 g
Sodium	224 mg

CHOCOLATE HUMMUS KISSED BY CRÈME DE CASSIS

Chocolate is a favourite flavour for French desserts. Why not bend the rules and have dessert hummus? Let's make it taste great, too. This dessert or snack will satisfy your sweet tooth and give you a boost of nutrients and protein. There's not much added sweetener, but it uses the best cocoa. Drizzle heavily with Crème de Cassis for a luxurious feel.

Yield: 3¼ cups (800 g),
14 servings
Total Time: 40 minutes
Equipment: Food processor, spatula

FLAVOURS: The intoxicating blend of chocolate and blackcurrant and the unique texture make this perfect for parties or a night in.

BENEFITS: Chickpeas are a good regulator of blood pressure and they have zero cholesterol. Low in saturated fat, high in protein and rich in fibre, you'll never feel guilty about eating this chocolate dessert.

2 tbsp (45 g) almond butter (or tahini)

4 tbsp (30 g) Dutch-processed cocoa

½ tsp low sodium tamari

½ tsp ground pepper

2 tbsp (41 ml) maple syrup or date syrup

18¼ oz (540 ml) chickpeas, canned, no salt added

4 tbsp (60 ml) filtered water

7 (85 g) strawberries (whole and sliced)

10 pistachios, crushed

dark chocolate, flaked

3–4 tbsp Crème de Cassis, for drizzling

Drain and rinse chickpeas. Place almond butter, cocoa, tamari, ground pepper, maple syrup and chickpeas in a food processor and blend on high for 1 minute.

Add water tablespoon by tablespoon and blend to achieve desired consistency.

Chill for 30 minutes. To garnish, add whole and sliced strawberries, crushed pistachios and flaked dark chocolate. Drizzle with Crème de Cassis. Use whole strawberries for dipping, or eat it with a spoon just like ice cream.

NUTRITION: *(per serving)*
4 tbsp (57 g) with ½ tsp Crème de Cassis

Calories	176
Fat	4.1 g
Saturated Fat	0.5 g
Cholesterol	0 mg
Carbohydrate	28.2 g
Fibre	7.8 g
Protein	8.5 g
Sugar	9 g
Sodium	27 mg

CHOCOLATE CHEESECAKE WITH GANACHE

This recipe will never be a health food, but if you are a chocoholic in need of a gluten-free option, this is your cake. Start with a deep, dark chocolate filling, then add dark rich chocolate ganache on top. The crust adds a sweetness, which is kicked up a notch with almond extract and more chocolate.

FLAVOURS: Pure dark chocolate with intoxicating flavours and aromas. The texture is creamy and the crust is nutty and sweet. Enough said!

BENEFITS: Compared to a traditional recipe, the calories are about 25% lower. Substitutions such as yoghurt and low-fat cream cheese help lower the total fat by about 20%. Total carbohydrates are reduced by 50% when using monk fruit. The carob adds calcium for bone health, and the crust has red maca to improve blood flow. While you may not eat it every day, it is a great alternative to a traditional cheesecake.

Yield: One 9" (23 cm) cheesecake, 12 servings
Total Time: 8 hours 30 minutes
Equipment: Springform pan, large baking pan, aluminum foil, mixing bowls, food processor, sharp knife

CRUST

1¾ cups + 2 tbsp (180 g) superfine almond flour
½ cup (50 g) toasted carob powder
3 tbsp (30 g) red maca
½ tsp almond extract
½ tsp monk fruit or ½ cup (115 g) sugar
4 tsp (10 g) unsweetened cocoa powder
7 tbsp (100 g) unsalted butter, melted

CRUST

Preheat oven to 325°F (163°C).

Grease the bottom and sides of a 9" (23 cm) springform pan. Wrap the outside of the pan in layers of heavy-duty aluminum foil. You'll be placing this pan in a water bath, so be sure the pan has been wrapped from every angle. Note: Test to make sure it is watertight by taking the empty pan and placing it into the pan of water.

In a medium mixing bowl, combine crust ingredients and the melted butter. Mix well. Pat the mixture firmly into the bottom of the prepared pan. Bake the crust for 15 minutes. Set the pan on a wire rack and cool the crust completely. Leave the oven on.

NUTRITION: *(per serving)*
7¾ oz (220 g)

Calories	593
Fat	48.7 g
Saturated Fat	29 g
Cholesterol	186 mg
Carbohydrate	25.4 g
Fibre	5.4 g
Protein	14.6 g
Sugar	18.5 g
Sodium	317 mg

CHOCOLATE CHEESECAKE FILLING

1 cup (180 g) bittersweet chocolate, coarsely chopped

¾ cup + 3 tbsp (160 g) Callebaut 70-30-38 dark chocolate or equivalent

24 oz (680 g) light cream cheese, at room temperature

3 tbsp (23 g) unsweetened cocoa powder

9¾ oz (275 g) Skyr 4% milk fat yoghurt

1 tbsp (13 ml) vanilla extract

¾ tsp monk fruit or ¾ cup (150 g) sugar

6 large eggs, room temperature

CHOCOLATE YOGHURT GANACHE

1 cup + 2 tbsp (226 g) Callebaut 70-30-38 dark chocolate, chopped

12 oz (340 g) Skyr 4% milk fat yoghurt

1½ tsp monk fruit or 2 cups (400 g) sugar

4 tbsp (57 g) unsalted butter, room temperature

¾ cup + 2 tbsp (110 g) raspberries, mashed

4 tbsp (57 g) unsalted butter, room temperature

CHOCOLATE CHEESECAKE FILLING

Fill a medium pot one-third full of water and bring it to a low simmer over medium heat.

Place a heatproof bowl that will fit snugly on top of the pan but not touch the simmering water. Reduce the heat to low and add the chopped chocolate into the bowl over the pot. Heat until the chocolate is completely melted, stirring occasionally with a silicone spatula. Remove the pot from the heat, leaving the bowl of chocolate over the hot water. Set aside until needed.

In the bowl of a food processor (or high-powered blender), pulse the cream cheese for about 2 minutes until completely smooth, scraping down the sides of the bowl as needed. Add the rest of the ingredients except the eggs and chocolate. Pulse for another minute. Add in the eggs and mix until just combined. Fold in the chocolate.

Remove the bowl from the food processor. Using a rubber spatula, stir the filling several times to ensure it's evenly blended.

Pour the filling over the partially baked crust.

Place the springform pan in a roasting pan or large baking pan filled with 1 inch (3 cm) of water. Place the roasting pan in the preheated oven.

Bake the cheesecake in the water bath for 1 hour and 10 minutes, or until the centre of the cake is set but still slightly jiggly. The cake will become more stable as it cools.

Remove the cake from the water bath and place the springform pan on a wire rack. Carefully loosen the foil from the outside of the pan. Cool completely (in the pan), then transfer the covered cheesecake to the refrigerator to chill for at least 6 hours before removing from the pan and slicing.

Before loosening the spring from the pan, carefully take a dull knife and run it around the inside of the pan to loosen the cake. Pull knife out often to clean before continuing to loosen the cake. Release the spring from the pan and remove. Set the covered cake aside in the refrigerator.

CHOCOLATE YOGURT GANACHE

Add chopped chocolate to a medium bowl. Set aside.

In a small saucepan over medium heat, bring the yoghurt to a low simmer. Do not overheat and scald it. Pour half of the yoghurt on top of the chocolate pieces and set aside for 1 minute. With a whisk, begin to incorporate the melted chocolate into the yoghurt. Slowly add the remaining yoghurt and continue whisking carefully until smooth and glossy.

Add in the butter and use a spatula to stir until the butter is completely melted. The mixture will be dark and glossy. Set aside, at room temperature, until needed.

Pour ganache over cooled cheesecake. Set aside until ganache is set, about 1 hour.

To serve, slice the cheesecake with a thin-bladed sharp knife, wiping the knife clean between each cut. Serve with fruit decorations or just dig in.

Store loosely covered in the refrigerator for up to 3 days.

DOUBLE CHOCOLATE FUDGE BROWNIES

These beauties have the consistency of a flourless cake but are all brownie when you bite into them. If you are feeling extra indulgent, drizzle with Crème de Cassis and watch them drip as you eat. The chocolate makes them irresistible, and the lower calorie count makes them a worthy substitute for traditional double chocolate fudge brownies.

Yield: 16 small brownies or 8 large brownies, 36 oz
Total Time: 45 minutes
Equipment: Nonstick 9" (23 cm) square pan, mixing bowls, whisk, wooden skewer

FLAVOURS: Deep dark chocolate flavour and aroma. The texture is moist and sinful!

BENEFITS: With zero cholesterol and 20% fewer calories using monkfruit in place of sugar, these are a great choice. The sunflower seed butter avoids tree-nut allergies with an added bonus of trace minerals such as copper and selenium, for bone and heart health.

4 heaped tbsp (64 g) unsweetened cocoa powder

½ tsp sea salt

1 tsp baking powder

¾ tsp instant espresso powder

3 flax "eggs" (see page 210)

2–6 tbsp (30–90 ml) filtered water

½ tbsp (7 ml) vanilla extract

½ cup (110 g) sunflower seed butter or almond butter

6 tbsp + ½ cup (207 ml) water

¾ tsp monk fruit or 1 cup (200 g) sugar

¾ cup + 2 tbsp (106 g) all-purpose unbleached white flour (organic preferred)

1½ cups (250 g) dark chocolate chips

¼–½ cup Crème de Cassis, for drizzling (optional)

blueberries or raspberries, for decoration (optional)

Preheat oven to 350°F (177°C).

Whisk the cocoa powder, salt, baking powder and espresso powder in a medium bowl. Add the flax "eggs", vanilla extract and 4 tbsp of water. Stir by hand (or use a hand mixer) until the batter has a satin sheen. Add more water (up to 2 tbsp) as needed. It will be thick.

Place the sunflower seed butter in a medium microwave-proof bowl and microwave for 30 seconds. Mix the monk fruit (or sugar) into the heated sunflower seed butter.

Add the hot sunflower seed mixture into the cocoa mixture and stir until smooth.

Set aside ⅓ cup (50 g) of the chocolate chips to sprinkle on top of the batter. Add the rest of the chocolate chips into the sunflower seed cocoa mixture and stir. Add the flour and water and mix until completely incorporated.

Spread the batter in the nonstick pan, as evenly as possible. Sprinkle the remaining chocolate chips on top.

Bake for 25–28 minutes or until a wooden skewer comes out clean or only a few crumbs cling to it. The brownies should be set on the edges, but moist in the middle (not unbaked).

Remove from oven and use a dull knife to spread the melted chocolate chips on top for a glossy finish. Let cool completely. Drizzle and decorate as desired. Cut and serve.

NUTRITION: *(per serving)*
1 small brownie, 2¼ oz (63 g)
monk fruit | sugar

Calories	161	208
Fat	9 g	
Saturated Fat	3.4 g	
Cholesterol	0 mg	
Carbohydrate	20.4 g	32.9 g
Fibre	1.9 g	
Protein	4.3 g	
Sugar	8.5 g	21 g
Sodium	14 mg	

The southerly view from the Basilique Notre-Dame de la Garde towards Marseille's Mediterranean coastline

It's Time
TO LEAVE

Small Changes, Big Changes

Dawn is near. I wake early. It's time for this journey to come to an end.

As I'm packing my bag, I sit down on the bedside and check the time. I've got a few minutes to spare. I don't want to lose this moment. Indulge me.

The beauty of travelling is that it provides an opportunity to reflect on our lives as we discover new places, people, traditions and, of course, food. I've been thinking about changes and how we adapt to them – big or small.

Flavour with Benefits was inspired by a five-year-old girl and the healing properties and nutritional value of an artichoke. The power of this lesson has become truer, as I see how the food I eat helps or hurts my health and the health of my family.

This trip has also highlighted that some changes in life may be dramatic and difficult while others are simple to make.

Reflecting on my love of La Belle France, I'm reminded about my family's many connections to this amazing country and an important gift given to the United States by the French people long ago. This gift represented hope for so many who gazed upon it for the first time.

BIG CHANGES – STATUES, FREEDOM AND A NEW LIFE

My son is an adult now, but at age 9, he won first place in a long-running children's art contest at the Arkansas Art Center in Little Rock, Arkansas. He painted his version of the Statue of Liberty (which I think has a cool vibe). The statue itself, located in New York Harbor, is steeped in symbolism, and it provides a fitting ending to this book.

It's a regal and impressive sight, inspired by Libertas – the Roman goddess of freedom. At the base of the statue's feet are broken shackles and chains. The statue has a foot raised as if moving forward. The torch represents enlightenment - and is held by a woman.

Two Frenchmen were central to creating *Liberté Éclairant le Monde* (Liberty Enlightening the World), known as the Statue of Liberty. The idea man was Édouard René de Laboulaye (1811–1883), who was a jurist, an anti-slavery activist and an admirer of the US Constitution, particularly the ideal of "liberty and justice for all". The sculptor was Frédéric Auguste Bartholdi (1834–1904). The statue was designed to celebrate the abolition of slavery in the United States. The monument was erected in 1886 on Bedloe Island (now known as Liberty Island). In 1889, the United States gave France a quarter-scale replica of the statue, which sits on an island in the middle of the Seine River at *Pont Grenelle* in Paris.

The symbolism of the Statue of Liberty soon welcomed new immigrants to America with the association of a poem used to raise money for the statue's pedestal. A bronze plaque of the poem "The New Colossus" by Emma Lazarus (1849–1887), written in 1883, was installed at the base of the statue in 1903. A famous phrase from the poem is, of course, "Give me your tired, your poor, Your huddled masses yearning to breathe free ..."

At the time the statue was first placed in New York's harbour, women could not vote anywhere in the world, yet Libertas still held the torch high. Between the intent of the statue and today's reality, much still remains to be done. Liberty, freedom, and enlightenment are a work-in-progress around the world.

We have come a long way, but for many, and those sadly gone, the statue's ideals and symbolism did not come fast enough. Life is imperfect, but we move forward. I suspect that Madame Clicquot and many of the women mentioned in this book would agree.

My maternal grandparents, Giovanna and Carlo, would each have sailed past the Statue of Liberty in the early 1900s as they immigrated to the United States. Their first steps in their new country were at Ellis Island – the first stop in the United States for over 12 million immigrants between 1892 and 1924. I wonder if, as they sailed into New York's harbour and passed the statue, they could imagine the challenges they would face: new country, new language, many children, including their oldest daughter, my mother, Mary. Who knew what the future would hold? But their lives in southern Italy were more complicated, and as hard as it was to leave, it was time to start a new life.

We will explore these stories in our next volume, *Flavour with Benefits: Sicily & Calabria*.

I hope you enjoyed this journey through magnificent France.

In honour of this wonderful country, I'd like to present one last recipe. It's a cheesecake. And the flavour? *Oh là là*. I give you "Vive la France!"

And now it's time to go. The stories of these courageous women and the images of beautiful places in France are timeless. Do try some of the recipes. My hope is that incremental nutritional changes, while never compromising on flavour, can improve your health, sexual vitality and happiness. And these changes provide a strong foundation and positive momentum for dealing with the challenges that life may put before us. Food should be our friend and ally.

Thanks again for reading *Flavour with Benefits: France*. Did you enjoy the book? What else would you like to see in future editions? Please leave a review and any suggestions you have on Amazon or Goodreads.

Calanque d'En-Vau Beach

Yield: One 8-inch (20 cm) cake, 8 slices
Total Time: 3–24 hours
Equipment: 8-inch (20 cm) springform pan, parchment paper, food processor, shower cap (or plastic wrap), dull knife, bowls

CRUST

¼ cup (56 g) unsweetened almond butter

scant ¾ cup (160 g) dates, diced

2–4 tbsp (30–60 ml) water

1 cup (115 g) superfine almond flour

FILLING

½ cup + 1 tbsp (150 g) unsweetened plant-based yoghurt (i.e. coconut or almond)

1 package (about 300 g) soft tofu (non-GMO), drained

24 oz (681 g) plant-based cream cheese (low or no added oil and low sodium)

3 tsp vanilla extract

1 tsp monk fruit
or ½ cup (100 g) sugar

TOPPING

1 apple (100 g), cored and diced

1 pear (178 g), cored and diced

½ cup (170 g) blueberries

heaping ½ cup (125 g) cherries, pitted and cut in half

2 tbsp (25 ml) lemon juice

This interpretation of the French flag using fresh fruits as the stripes, is a tribute to the role that agriculture plays in France. The natural flavours and sweetness of these fruits bring this plant-based cheesecake to life. It does not compromise on the creamy texture which is fundamental to this classic cake. With coconut yoghurt, plant-based cream cheese and soft tofu in place of dairy and eggs, it will tantalize your tastebuds.

FLAVOURS: Traditional vanilla complemented by a creamy texture that leaves you wanting more. Fresh fruits like blueberries, apples, pears and sweet cherries provide a different flavour in every bite. Dates and almonds in the crust give a nice finish of sweetness and nutty flavours.

BENEFITS: The saturated fats are 75% lower than a traditional cheesecake. You also get a calorie reduction of 25%, lower net carbohydrates and a boost of fibre. Tofu makes the cake high in protein and calcium, and the fruits add antioxidants, vitamins and minerals.

CRUST

Preheat oven to 350°F (177°C).
Mix dates and water in a medium-sized bowl and microwave for 30 seconds. Mix the dates until soft and incorporate them fully. If the dates are somewhat dry, add 2 more tablespoons of water and microwave for 30 seconds. Add the nut or seed butter and almond flour and mix well until it forms a paste. Put parchment paper on the bottom of the springform pan. Use a piece large enough to extend well over the outside edges when you press the spring in place. This allows for easy release later. Press the mixture evenly and smoothly into the bottom of the pan. Bake for 12–15 minutes until brown and firm. Set aside.

FILLING

Mix all filling ingredients in the food processor. Purée for 2–3 minutes until completely smooth. Pour mixture into the springform pan with the previously baked crust. Smooth the top with a spatula. Bake for 30–35 minutes.

It should be firm on the edges but still slightly jiggly in the centre. Do not overbake. Let cool on counter or hot pad for 1–2 hours. Refrigerate for at least 2 hours until completely cool. Use plastic wrap or shower cap to cover cake in refrigerator to prevent drying out. Use a wet, dull knife and loosen the edge of the cake before loosening the springform pan.

TOPPING

Place diced apples and pears into a bowl with lemon juice with 2 cups of water until ready for use. This prevents browning. If your cake has cracked on top, use a spatula to fill in the cracks with either cream cheese or yoghurt. Place decorative fruit on top in desired pattern. Cut and serve.

NUTRITION: *(per serving)*
1 slice, 9¼ oz (265 g)
with monk fruit | with sugar

	with monk fruit	with sugar
Calories	382	429
Fat	20.4 g	
Saturated Fat	4.8 g	
Cholesterol	0 mg	
Carbohydrate	42.7 g	55.2 g
Fibre	6.6 g	
Protein	6.4 g	
Sugar	23 g	35.5 g
Sodium	320 mg	

Flavour with Benefits

SICILY & CALABRIA PREVIEW

The "ghost town" of Pentedattilo, Calabria, Italy

Praetorian Fountain in the Piazza Pretoria plaza in Palermo, Sicily. Built in 1554 in Florence but later transported to Palermo in 644 pieces in 1574.

Doric-style Greek Temple of Segesta built by the Elmyians near Calatafimi, Sicily

Lasagna Verde with Asparagus

My maternal grandparents, Giovanna and Carlo Rogolino, from Reggio, Calabria with their oldest son, Antonino

My Sicilian Kiwi Sorbet – so good on a hot Sicilian day

Drone view of pool in Collesano, Sicily

Resources
AND TOOLS

Recipe Index & Profiles

This provides a quick index of recipes with various informational attributes. This may help in your recipe selections. The legend and additional notes are on the last page of this profile.

Recipe Description	Page	Time	Difficulty	Veg	Vegan	Zero Cholesterol	Oil-Free	Sugar-Free	High Fibre Source	Gluten-free	Tree-Nut Free	Enhances Sexual Vitality
Artichoke Hummus	51	45 minutes	Easy	X	X	X	X	X	X	X	X (Note 1)	X
Artichokes (Steamed) with Mustard Sauce	48	35 minutes	Easy	X		X	X	X	X	X	X	X
Asparagus (Steamed) with "Hollandaise" Sauce	52	15 minutes	Easy	X	X	X	X	X	X	X	X	X
Asparagus (Steamed) with "Cheese" Sauce	132	35 minutes	Easy	X	X	X	X	X	X	X		X
Baguette (Classic)	171	20 hours	Moderate	X	X	X	X	X	X		X	
Banana Bread (Classic)	85	1 hour 30 minutes	Easy	X	X	X	X	X	X		X (Note 1) (Note 2)	X
Biscuit Rose de Reims	29	50 minutes	Moderate	X							X	
Blueberry (Maple) Deep-Dish Pie (A Tribute to Vincent Van Gogh: *The Starry Night*)	140	2-3 hours	Advanced	X							X	
Carob Apricot Whole Wheat Sourdough Bread	35	20 to 32 hours	Advanced	X	X	X	X	X	X		X	X
Cashew (Cultured) "Cheese"	32	2 ½ days	Moderate	X	X	X	X	X		X		X
Cauliflower Steak on Cauliflower Potato Soup	110	1 hour 30 minutes	Moderate	X	X	X	X	X	X	X	X (Note 1)	X
Cherry Clafoutis	146	1 hour 45 minutes	Easy	X						X	X (Note 3)	
Chicken (Roasted Spatchcock) and Vegetables	77	1 hour 30 minutes	Moderate					X	X	X	X	
Chocolate Cheesecake with Chocolate Ganache	180	8 hours 30 minutes	Advanced	X						X	X (Note 3)	
Chocolate Donuts with Chocolate Frosting	86	1 hour 15 minutes	Moderate	X	X	X	X		X		X (Note 1)	X
Chocolate (Double) Fudge Brownies	185	45 minutes	Easy	X	X	X	X		X		X	X
Chocolate Hummus Kissed by Crème de Cassis	179	40 minutes	Easy	X	X	X	X		X	X	X (Note 1) (Note 2)	X

Recipe Description	Page	Time	Difficulty	Veg	Vegan	Zero Cholesterol	Oil-Free	Sugar-Free	High Fibre Source	Gluten-free	Tree Nut Free	Enhances Sexual Vitality
Chocolate Mousse – Avocado Surprise	105	15 minutes	Easy	X	X	X	X		X	X	X	X
Coffee-Rub (Grilled) Ribeye Steak	130	45 minutes	Easy				X			X		
Cornbread (Dad and Stella's) Recipe with a Surprise	82	35 minutes	Easy	X					X		X	
Crêpes (Ancient)	106	2 hours 45 minutes	Easy	X	X	X	X	X	X	X	X	X
Crudités with Dipping Sauce	73	20 minutes	Easy	X		X	X			X	X	
French Fries (Baked) (Frites au Four)	168	40 minutes	Easy	X	X	X	X	X	X	X	X	X
French Onion Soup – A Classic Revisited	163	2 hours 15 minutes	Moderate	X	X	X	X		X		X (Note 4)	X
Potatoes au Gratin (Gratin Dauphinois)	137	1 hour	Easy	X	X	X	X	X	X	X		X
Kale, (Crunchy) Fennel & Cabbage Salad	31	20 minutes	Easy	X	X	X	X	X	X	X	X	X
Lavender Blueberry Dressing for a Summer Salad	134	15 minutes	Easy	X	X	X	X	X		X	X (Note 1)	X
Leek Potato Onion & Edamame Soup	74	45 minutes	Easy	X	X	X	X	X	X	X	X	X
Lemon Cake (Gâteau d'Arles)	138	50 minutes	Moderate	X	X	X	X	X	X		X	X
Lemon Lavender Luxury Cheesecake	145	3 hours	Easy	X						X	X (Note 3)	
Pears (Festive Poached Beaujolais)	102	1 hour	Moderate	X	X	X	X	X	X	X	X	X
Pear Raspberry Quinoa Salad with Aged Balsamic Vinegar	109	15 minutes	Easy	X	X	X	X	X	X	X	X (Note 2)	X
Plum and Cherry Torte	56	1 hour 15 minutes	Easy	X				X	X		X	
Potato Salad (French)	113	50 minutes	Easy	X	X	X	X	X	X	X	X	X
Quiche Lorraine Nue (Naked Quiche Lorraine)	55	1 hour	Easy	X				X	X	X	X	
Raspberry Oatmeal Bars	59	45 minutes	Easy	X	X	X	X		X			X
Rhubarb Tart	149	1 hour	Advanced	X	X	X	X	X	X	X		X
Salad Niçoise Inspired by Julia Child	164	45 minutes	Moderate	X	X	X	X		X	X	X	X
Sea Bass Cassis	167	20 minutes	Easy							X	X	
Strawberry Rhubarb Champagne Cheesecake	24	3 hours 30 minutes	Moderate	X						X	X (Note 3)	
Sweet Potatoes (Fancy Piped)	114	45 minutes	Easy	X	X	X	X	X	X	X	X	X
Sweet Potato Fries	81	35 minutes	Easy	X	X	X	X	X	X	X	X	X

Recipe Description	Page	Time	Difficulty	Veg	Vegan	Zero Cholesterol	Oil-Free	Sugar-Free	High Fibre Source	Gluten-free	Tree Nut Free	Enhances Sexual Vitality
Sweet Potato Walnut Bread (French Country)	175	20 hours	Moderate	X	X	X	X	X	X		X (Note 2)	X
Tétons de Vénus Cakes	98	2 to 3 hours	Advanced	X					X			
Viva La France Cheesecake	192	3 to 24 hours	Moderate	X	X	X	X		X	X		X
Zoodles (Sautéed) with Sweet Pepper Purée	133	30 minutes	Moderate	X	X	X	X	X	X	X	X	X
ALTERNATIVE INGREDIENTS RECIPES												
Applesauce - Unsweetened	204	15 minutes	Easy	X	X	X	X	X	X	X	X	X
"Beef" Broth	204	1 hour 10 minutes	Easy	X	X	X	X	X		X	X	X
Buttermilk - Substitute	205	10 minutes	Easy	X	X	X	X	X		X	X	X
"Cheese" Sauce	206	40 minutes	Easy	X	X	X	X	X	X	X		X
Crystallised Ginger	207	1 hour	Moderate	X		X	X		X	X	X	
Date Purée	208	15 minutes	Easy	X	X	X	X	X	X	X	X	X
Flax "Eggs"	210	7 minutes	Easy	X	X	X	X	X	X	X	X	X
"Gruyère Cheese"	211	20 minutes	Easy	X	X	X	X	X	X	X	X	X
Hard Boiled "Eggs" (*Faux Oeuf Dur*)	209	5 hours 30 minutes	Advanced	X	X	X	X	X	X	X	X	X
"Parmesan Cheese"	212	5 minutes	Easy	X	X	X	X	X	X	X		X
Sugar Revisited (Decorating)	208	5 minutes	Easy	X		X	X			X	X	
Sweet Potato Purée	213	45 minutes	Easy	X	X	X	X	X	X	X	X	X
"Worcestershire" Sauce	214	10 minutes	Easy	X	X	X	X	X		X	X	X

Note 1: Tahini or sunflower seed butter can be substituted for almond butter one for one to avoid a tree nut allergy.

Note 2: Eliminate nuts for tree nut allergy.

Note 3: Oat or tigernut flour could be used in lieu of almond flour.

Note 4: Eliminate the vegan cheese as it has cashews.

TERMS USED IN TABLE

DIFFICULTY
Easy, Moderate and Advanced. This is based on the number of steps that a recipe takes and/or the number of ingredients or recipes included.

TIME
Total time to prepare and cook or bake. When a main recipe references an alternative ingredient recipe, the time shown is total time including preparation of the alternative ingredient recipe.

VEG
Vegetarian with no meat but includes foods with dairy and eggs.

VEGAN
No meat, eggs or dairy but could include added oil of any type.

ZERO CHOLESTEROL
Plant-based foods such as fruits, vegetables, legumes and whole grains.

OIL-FREE
No added extracted/pressed oil of any type.

SUGAR-FREE
Use of natural plant-based sweeteners such as dates, monk fruit and stevia.

HIGH FIBRE SOURCE
Any serving that is at least 10% of the average recommended daily fibre requirement for women, which is 25 grams per day.

GLUTEN-FREE
Uses no wheat-based products in the recipe.

TREE NUT-FREE
Uses no tree nuts or suggests ways to eliminate them from the recipe to make them nut-free.

ENHANCES SEXUAL VITALITY
Any recipe that is high fibre, zero cholesterol, oil-free and vegan because much of sexual vitality is related to heart health and adequate blood flow.

Alternative Ingredients Recipes

APPLESAUCE - UNSWEETENED

This recipe is a good homemade applesauce that can be used in place of oil, in some baking recipes. You can make it as smooth as you wish or more rustic by leaving the skins on. It may brown quickly depending on what type of apples you use, but if you're baking quick breads, it may not matter as the bread will be brown anyway.

Yield: 2½ cups (300 g)
Total Time: 15 minutes
Equipment: Food processor

2 apples (185 g), cored, diced

FLAVOURS: Fresh, naturally sweet apple flavour. Great for baking.

BENEFITS: Saves money and there is no added sugar. Unpeeled organic apples are high in fibre, vitamins A, C and K, as well as minerals such as calcium and potassium.

If the apples are organic, leave the skins on. Place into food processor and purée until very smooth. Add ¼ to ½ cup water to achieve smooth consistency.

NUTRITION: *(per serving)*
2½ cups (300 g)

Calories	215
Fat	0.7 g
Saturated Fat	0 g
Cholesterol	0 mg
Carbohydrate	57 g
Fibre	10 g
Protein	1.1 g
Sugar	42.9 g
Sodium	4 mg

"BEEF" BROTH

This recipe uses some tricks to emulate a favourite "Beef Broth", but is plant-based and takes about an hour to make. It can also be stored for later use.

Yield: 2½ cups (620 ml)
Total Time: 1 hour 10 minutes
Equipment: Large pot

2¼ cups (535 ml) low sodium vegetable broth

¼ cup (60 ml) red wine

2½ tbsp (40 ml) soy sauce or tamari

1 tbsp (17 g) "Worcestershire" sauce (see page 214)

1 tsp dried thyme

1 tsp onion powder

1 tsp ground cumin

¼–½ tsp ground black pepper

FLAVOURS: Red wine, garlic, onion and tangy Worcestershire give you that hint of beef flavour.

BENEFITS: Vegan and low in sodium, with trace amounts of calcium.

Place all ingredients in a large pot and simmer for an hour on low heat. Remove from heat and allow to cool.

NUTRITION: *(per serving)*
1 cup (236 ml)

Calories	29
Fat	0 g
Saturated Fat	0 g
Cholesterol	0 mg
Carbohydrate	3.4 g
Fibre	0.2 g
Protein	0.7 g
Sugar	1.4 g
Sodium	370 mg

BUTTERMILK - SUBSTITUTE

This recipe is for those times you need real buttermilk, but you don't have it on hand. Your grandmother probably told you about using vinegar and milk, but this version has an added ingredient that emulates the thickness of buttermilk.

Yield: 1¼ cups (360 g)
Total Time: 10 minutes
Equipment: Bowl, spoon

1 cup (340 g) unsweetened plant-based milk, almond milk or soy milk

1 tsp vinegar (apple cider vinegar preferred)

1 tbsp (15 g) plain plant-based unsweetened yoghurt

FLAVOURS: You guessed it, pretty much like buttermilk.

BENEFITS: Zero cholesterol and lower in sugar and sodium. It can be made at a moment's notice. It is also helpful for most of us over the age of 20 who are lactose intolerant. While it is lower in protein, this is fine, as the average woman consumes much more protein than needed.

Mix all ingredients thoroughly and let stand for 10 minutes before using.

Refrigerate until needed.

NUTRITION: *(per serving)*
1¼ cup (360 g)
buttermilk sub. | full fat buttermilk

Calories	190 | 190
Fat	10 g | 10.1 g
Saturated Fat	5.9 g | 5.9 g
Cholesterol	0 mg | 34 mg
Carbohydrate	17.4 g | 15 g
Fibre	1.5 g | 0 g
Protein	1.5 g | 9.9 g
Sugar	10.2 g | 15 g
Sodium	130 mg | 321 mg

"CHEESE" SAUCE

Cheese is a much-loved food around the world, but it is a way of life in France. This plant-based sauce gives you a cheesy taste without the calories or cholesterol. The flavour is deep and rich and can be varied by adding more garlic, lemon or nutritional yeast.

Yield: 6 servings, 4½ cups (560 g)
Total Time: 40 minutes
Equipment: Pot, sharp knife, grater, food processor

½ cup (75 g) raw cashews

1 baked Russet potato, (170 g)

½ cup (75 g) onion, chopped

1 tbsp (10 g) fresh turmeric, grated, or 1 tsp turmeric powder

5 cloves garlic (25 g), pressed

1 large carrot (75 g), chopped

1–2 tsp smoked paprika

½–¾ cup (30–45 g) nutritional yeast (to taste)

1 tsp tamari or soy sauce

½ tsp freshly ground black pepper

2½ cups (590 ml) filtered water

FLAVOURS: Somewhere between a Monterey Jack and a newer cheddar cheese with some added creaminess from the unexpected ingredient, mashed potatoes.

BENEFITS: This is a low-calorie alternative to a traditional cheese sauce. The anti-inflammatory properties of turmeric, along with the huge whack of B vitamins and minerals, make this one a winner. There is also a nice dose of fibre.

Place cashews in a small bowl and cover them with water. Soak for 20 minutes. Discard water.

Put baked potato, onions, fresh turmeric (not turmeric powder), garlic, carrot and 2 cups filtered water into a medium pot or saucepan. Bring to a boil. Reduce heat to low and simmer for about 15 minutes.

Put cashews and potato mixture (and dried turmeric, if using) into a food processor. Add smoked paprika, nutritional yeast, tamari and freshly ground pepper and blend for 30 seconds. Add ½ cup of water (or more) a little at a time until you get the desired level of thickness. Blend for up to 2 minutes or until smooth.

Serve over vegetables or with pasta such as macaroni.

Thank you to *The China Study Family Cookbook* for inspiration for this recipe. It was reprinted with permission from the T. Colin Campbell Center for Nutrition Studies (nutritionstudies.org).

NUTRITION: *(per serving)*
6 tbsp (93 g)

Calories	109
Fat	5.5 g
Saturated Fat	1.1 g
Cholesterol	0 mg
Carbohydrate	12.7 g
Fibre	2.2 g
Protein	3.9 g
Sugar	1.7 g
Sodium	69 mg

CRYSTALLISED GINGER (HOMEMADE)

This recipe gives you a fragrant and fresh version of crystallised ginger that is better than the store-bought variety. It is quite magical to see the sugar crystals forming as it cooks and cools.

Yield: 1½ cups (220 g)
Total Time: 1 hour
Equipment: Mandoline, knife, cooling rack, saucepan

2 cups (200 g) ginger root, fresh

½ cup (100 g) granulated sugar

2 cups (473 ml) filtered water

FLAVOURS: Pure ginger with its natural heat offset by extremely sweet crystallised sugar.

BENEFITS: Fresh ginger has anti-inflammatory properties. Due to the amount of sugar in this recipe it could be argued that health benefits are very low, but it doesn't hurt to have a treat once in awhile.

Prepare a cooling rack with parchment paper.

Peel the ginger root. Using a knife or a mandoline, cut ginger into ⅛" (3 mm) slices.

Put water into a medium saucepan and place ginger into the pan. Cook over medium-high heat. Cover and cook for 20–25 minutes or until ginger is soft.

Put a bowl underneath a colander and drain the ginger. Retain a quarter of the ginger water. Weigh the ginger and measure out an equal amount of sugar. Return the ginger water and sugar to the saucepan.

Bring to a boil over medium-high heat, stirring frequently until sugar syrup is dry. After about 20 minutes, it should be evaporated and begin to recrystallise. Watch carefully. It will change quickly.

Separate the ginger pieces and place them on the cooling rack. Set aside the remaining ginger sugar water for use with Festive Beaujolais Poached Pears (page 102).

Use ginger right away or store in a sealed container for a few weeks. It can also be frozen.

NUTRITION: *(per serving)*
4 pieces (~42 g)

Calories	125
Fat	0 g
Saturated Fat	0 g
Cholesterol	0 mg
Carbohydrate	32.5 g
Fibre	0.8 g
Protein	0.7 g
Sugar	13.8 g
Sodium	13 mg

DATE PURÉE

Who doesn't love dates? They can be used in many recipes as a stand-in for sugar, and they add some welcome creamy texture too.

FLAVOURS: A smooth texture and added sweetness for your baked goods.

BENEFITS: Fibre-rich and high in copper, manganese, iron, potassium and vitamin B6 make this fruit a powerhouse and a great substitute for sugar in many recipes.

Yield: 2¼ cups (500 g)
Total Time: 15 minutes
Equipment: Pan, food processor

2 cups (380 g) dates

1 cup (237 ml) filtered water

Cook the dates and water in a saucepan on low to medium heat until tender. Stir a few times. They should be cooked in 10 minutes. Drain and reserve water.

Put date mixture in blender or food processor with maple syrup and date sugar. Add just enough of the date water to make a creamy consistency. It should be somewhat thick. Set aside.

Recipe reprinted with permission from the T. Colin Campbell Center for Nutrition Studies (nutritionstudies.org).

NUTRITION: *(per serving)*
3½ oz (100 g)

Calories	214
Fat	0.3 g
Saturated Fat	0 g
Cholesterol	0 mg
Carbohydrate	57 g
Fibre	6.1 g
Protein	1.9 g
Sugar	48.2 g
Sodium	2 mg

DECORATING SUGAR REVISITED

Sprinkling icing or confectioners' sugar on a dessert gives it a festive look, but it can add empty carbohydrates and calories depending on how heavily it is applied.

FLAVOURS: Icing sugar with just a little less sweetness but it's difficult to taste the difference when used to decorate desserts.

BENEFITS: This trick will give you the same look with 40% fewer calories and 50% less sugar.

Yield: 1 cup
Total Time: 5 minutes
Equipment: Whisk, small bowl, icing sugar duster

½ cup (50 g) icing sugar

½ cup (64 g) arrowroot starch

Whisk ingredients together and put into a sugar dispenser.

NUTRITION: *(per serving)*
1 cup | 1 cup icing sugar

Calories	272	467
Fat	0.2 g	0.1 g
Saturated Fat	0 g
Cholesterol	0 mg
Carbohydrate	67.8 g	119.5 g
Fibre	0.8 g	0 g
Protein	2.5 g	0 g
Sugar	58.8 g	117.5 g
Sodium	16 mg	1 mg

FAUX OEUFS DURS (HARD BOILED "EGGS")

These are a fun substitute when you want that boiled egg look in a vegan meal. It takes some time, but the results are beautiful. You can use this on top of a Salad Niçoise to emulate egg. The yolk packs a punch, though!

Yield: 10-12 half eggs
Total Time: 5 hours 30 minutes
Equipment: Saucepan, food processor, egg-shaped silicone forms

FLAVOURS: The eggy taste comes from black salt and the Dijon mustard gives you some heat.

BENEFITS: Packed with fibre, vitamins and calcium. It's also vegan, plus low in fat.

"EGG" WHITE BASE

1 cup (200 g) navy beans

4 cups (237 ml) water

"EGG" WHITE

heaping ½ cup (160 g) cooked navy beans

½ cup (116 ml) water

1 tsp arrowroot starch

1 tsp tapioca flour

"EGG" YOLK

¾ cup (150 g) canned cannellini beans, drained

3¾ tsp arrowroot starch

1½ tsp Dijon mustard

pinch of Himalayan black salt

¼ tsp garlic powder

¼ tsp turmeric powder

"EGG" WHITE BASE

Soak the beans for 3 hours in lukewarm water until soft.

After soaking, simmer the beans for 20 minutes.

Drain and set aside. These will be used to make the "egg" white.

"EGG" WHITE
Put all ingredients into the food processor and blend until smooth.

"EGG" YOLK
Put all ingredients into the food processor and blend until smooth.

ASSEMBLY
Preheat oven to 350°F (177°C).

Put egg-shaped silicone form onto a cookie sheet. Press 18–20 grams of "egg" white into the form. This will vary depending on the size of your form. You want to get the white covering the entire inside of the form and leave a well for the yolk in the middle.

Press 10–12 grams of "egg" yolk into the well of the "egg" white. Take care not to punch through the egg white on the bottom of the form.

Smooth the top with a knife.

Put into oven and bake for 10-15 minutes until set but not hard. Do not overcook as they will crack and dry out too much. Chill for at least 1–2 hours. Remove carefully from the silicone moulds. Level the half eggs with a sharp knife to get a smooth edge, much like a hard-boiled egg.

NUTRITION: *(per serving)*
½ "egg" (90 g)

Calories	102
Fat	0.3 g
Saturated Fat	0.1 g
Cholesterol	0 mg
Carbohydrate	18.5 g
Fibre	7.1 g
Protein	6.6 g
Sugar	0.9 g
Sodium	20 mg

FLAX "EGGS"

These can be used as a substitute for eggs in baking. They are simple to make and ready in minutes. The only time these may not be optimal is if you have a white or light-coloured batter as the flecks of gold may show up. But you can colour the batter with strawberries or a similar fruit to mask that easily. It's amazing how versatile these are as a substitution, especially when you add leavening agents like baking powder, baking soda or yeast to a recipe.

Yield: 1 flax "egg"
Total time: 7 minutes
Equipment: Bowl, tablespoon

1 tbsp (10 g) ground flaxseed*

3 tbsp (15 ml) warm water

FLAVOURS: You don't make these for their flavour. They are basically tasteless in the quantities used, which is helpful in many recipes. They allow other flavours to flourish.

BENEFITS: Compared to regular eggs, flax "eggs" have 30% fewer calories, zero cholesterol, almost no saturated fats and are fibre rich. To top it off, flaxseed is high in omega-3s, which are great for your heart and assist in reducing hypertension.

Mix flax seed and water together in a small bowl and let sit for 5 minutes. Stir a few times. It will set and have a gel-like quality like an egg. If your recipe depends on an eggy taste, you add a dash of Himalayan black salt (which has sulphur) to provide the egg-like taste.

*Preferably golden or yellow flaxseed, but if that is not available, ground brown flaxseed can be used. It just may take slightly longer for it to absorb the water.

NUTRITION: *(per serving)*
1 flax "egg" (25 g) | 1 large egg

Calories	51 | 72
Fat	3.3 g | 5 g
Saturated Fat	0.3 g | 1.6 g
Cholesterol	0 mg | 186 mg
Carbohydrate	3.3 g | 0.4 g
Fibre	2.7g | 0 g
Protein	1.9 g | 6.3 g
Sugar	0 g | 0.4g
Sodium	3 mg | 70 mg

"GRUYÈRE CHEESE"

Who says "cheese" has to take a long time to make? This stand-in for Gruyère tastes great, and the consistency is ideal for dishes such as French Onion Soup (page 163).

Yield: 12 servings, 1½ cups (337 g)
Total time: 20 minutes
Equipment: Blender, saucepan, whisk

1 cup (237 ml) water
2 tbsp (29 ml) apple cider vinegar
2 tbsp (30 ml) tahini paste
2 tbsp +1 tsp (11 g) nutritional yeast
5 tsp (21 g) arrowroot starch or cornstarch
2 tbsp (13 g) rolled oats (quick or large flakes)
1 tsp garlic powder
2 tsp onion powder
½ tsp tamari, soy sauce or sea salt

FLAVOURS: The salty, tangy notes of this cheese will have you reaching for seconds. The oats also give it a nice texture.

BENEFITS: This poser comes in at 40% fewer calories, 75% less saturated fat, and less than half the sodium. Worth a try to see what you think.

Put all ingredients into the food processor or blender and blend for 30 seconds to a minute until smooth.

Pour ingredients into a small saucepan over medium heat. Whisk constantly until the mixture thickens to your desired consistency. If you drag the whisk into the mixture and let it fall, it should be somewhat stretchy and thicker. This should take about 3–5 minutes.

Remove from heat and continue whisking for about 2–3 minutes. Let cool before use for 10 minutes or store in the refrigerator.

Note: The reason we use a whisk instead of a spoon or spatula is because the mixture will develop lumps. But even if you do get lumps, it will taste great.

Thank you to WikiHow for recipe inspiration.

NUTRITION: *(per serving)*
2 tbsp (28 g)

Calories	33
Fat	1.5 g
Saturated Fat	0.2 g
Cholesterol	0 mg
Carbohydrate	3.6 g
Fibre	0.9 g
Protein	1.7 g
Sugar	0.2 g
Sodium	17 mg

"PARMESAN CHEESE"

If you crave the flavour of cheese without the calories, this recipe might give you something to cheer about. Sprinkle this on salads and anything else you add Parmesan to, such as French Onion Soup.

Yield: 20 servings 1¼ cup (320 g)
Total Time: 5 minutes
Equipment: Food processor

1 cup (150 g) raw cashews
2-3 garlic cloves (15-20 g) (taste after 2 and see if it needs more)
3 tsp fresh squeezed lemon juice
½ cup (88 g) nutritional yeast
1 tsp tamari
½ tsp fine sea salt
3 tsp garlic powder
2 tsp onion powder

FLAVOURS: The salty, nutty and tangy notes of this cheese will not fool you but will add a nice texture and finish to dishes that call for it.

BENEFITS: No reduction in calories, but this version has zero cholesterol, is lower in sodium, has some fibre and is also dairy-free.

Blend all ingredients in food processor and add additional amounts to taste. Serve immediately. It will keep in the refrigerator for a week.

NUTRITION: *(per serving)*
1 tbsp (16 g)

Calories	56
Fat	3.4 g
Saturated Fat	0.7 g
Cholesterol	0 mg
Carbohydrate	4.7 g
Fibre	1.3 g
Protein	3 g
Sugar	0.7 g
Sodium	67 mg

SWEET POTATO PURÉE

This can be used as a side dish or as a part of baked goods such as donuts. Fast and healthy. If using as a snack, add cinnamon and mace to give it sweet aromas and spice.

Yield: ½ cup, (100 g)
Total Time: 45 minutes
Equipment: Pan, food processor

1 to 1½ (150 g raw) sweet potatoes, washed

FLAVOURS: The sweet taste of a freshly baked sweet potato is a wonderful one all by itself.

BENEFITS: A highly nutritious vegetable packed with fibre, protein, potassium, complex carbohydrates and vitamins C and B.

Preheat oven to 425°F (218°C). Line a pan with foil.

Cut a small amount off the ends to prevent bursting.

Bake with skins on for 40-45 minutes. Check doneness with fork.

Peel skins off when cool enough to handle, or use a fork. Do not discard skins. They have a lot of food value. Use them in a salad or soup. Puree the sweet potatoes in a blender or food processor. Sweet potatoes may shrink by 20% in weight in baking.

NUTRITION: *(per serving)*
½ cup cooked (100 g)

Calories	103
Fat	0.2 g
Saturated Fat	0 g
Cholesterol	0 mg
Carbohydrate	23.6 g
Fibre	3.8 g
Protein	2.3 g
Sugar	7.4 g
Sodium	41 mg

"WORCESTERSHIRE" SAUCE

This plant-based recipe is more affordable than the original Worcestershire sauce, which has anchovies.

Yield: ¾ cup (350 g)
Total Time: 10 minutes
Equipment: Saucepan

1 cup (193 ml) apple cider vinegar

⅓ cup (80 ml) low sodium soy sauce or tamari

3 tbsp (54 g) date sugar or brown sugar

1 tsp Dijon mustard

½ tsp allspice

1 tsp garlic powder

1 tsp onion powder

⅛ tsp ground black pepper

FLAVOURS: This is a tough one. You guessed it, Worcestershire sauce. It's a lovely sauce that balances the sweet and tangy notes.

BENEFITS: Fewer calories and lower sodium gives this sauce an advantage. It's vegan and can be easily made at home affordably.

Place all ingredients into a medium saucepan and cover. Whisk ingredients to eliminate any lumps and to fully incorporate all ingredients. Heat on low until a low simmer. Cook for 3-5 minutes.

Remove from heat and cool to room temperature. Store in a tightly covered jar in the refrigerator. Will keep for up to a month.

Thank you to Karissa's Vegan Kitchen for inspiration for this recipe.

NUTRITION: *(per serving)*
1 tbsp (30 g)

Calories	10
Fat	0 g
Saturated Fat	0 g
Cholesterol	0 mg
Carbohydrate	1.9 g
Fibre	0.1 g
Protein	0.2 g
Sugar	1.4 g
Sodium	132 mg

Tools for Your Kitchen

To make your food journey efficient and more enjoyable, some kitchen tools are essential. They don't have to be expensive, but you do need a few to get the job done. Without them, it may take longer to make your favourite dish, and some may not work as well as you had hoped. Cooking and baking should be fun and easy, and these tools help make that a reality.

KITCHEN BASICS:

BPA-FREE STORAGE CONTAINERS	Leftovers can be stored and used in the next meal. Having good storage containers is essential to cut costs and work and lower food waste.
BROTFORM PROOFING BASKETS	Also called banneton baskets, are used for shaping dough during warm or cold fermentation. They must be seasoned first using rice flour to prevent sticking.
CAST-IRON PAN	This pan is old school and a wonderful tool for oil-free cooking. It takes a bit of time to heat, but it keeps an even temperature and cooks at high temperatures. It can also be used to bake pizzas, cakes, etc. A good size is 9–10" (23–25 cm).
CUTTING BOARD(S)	You may want a high-quality wooden cutting board that has non-slip rubber on the bottom. Wooden boards initially require a day or two of seasoning with mineral oil, but from then on, they are good to go. If you get a thick one (say 2–3" or 5–8 cm), they will draw any impurities down into the wood. Clean daily with warm soap and water. To disinfect, use hydrogen peroxide. Another option is plastic cutting boards that can be put into the dishwasher, but they will need to be replaced fairly often as the crevices may collect dirt that is hard to remove. Always use a cutting board to protect your knives.
FOOD PROCESSOR or BLENDER	Absolutely essential for food preparation. It makes quick work of so many tasks. You can even shred veggies such as carrots or zucchini. Get a good one. They are not too expensive, and you can usually find them on sale.
GARLIC PRESS	A kitchen essential that helps spread garlic out in cooked dishes but also releases the sulphur compounds when crushed or pressed, which improves heart health.
GRATER	Useful to grate vegetables, turmeric or ginger.
IMMERSION BLENDER	This is such a clever tool. It is basically a blender on a stick that can be immersed in a soup, for example, to blend it without transferring it to a food processor. It can be used on hot or cold substances.
KNIVES	There are three types of knives that are essential. The first is a high-quality chef knife, preferably 8" (20 cm), with a blade that can be sharpened (if you use metal). You will need a knife-steel to keep the edge sharp. Videos on YouTube can help with this technique. Take your knives to a professional to sharpen every two years. Ceramic knives are good too, but they may not last as long. The second is a paring knife for cutting or peeling smaller items. The third is a bread knife. If you eat bread, you need this knife too. Bread knives don't need sharpening. Keep your knives in a knife block and do not wash them in a dishwasher as they will lose their edge.

LAME	This is a tool used by bakers to cut or "score" the top of bread in various designs.
MEASURING CUPS	Some people are shy about scales, so you can use measuring cups instead. For wet ingredients, you can use a larger clear glass or plastic or quarter-litre version.
MEASURING SPOONS	These are essential and will be used almost every day. If you can get a set with ¾ and ⅛ teaspoons, that is even better to make some measuring tasks easier.
NONSTICK PANS (STAINLESS OR CERAMIC COATED)	These pans are a great way to sauté veggies without oil and for baking. You should use silicone or wooden utensils so the surface is not damaged. I don't recommend Teflon as it is easy to scratch and may release toxic chemicals when this happens.
OVEN MITTS	Heavy silicone mitts that cover wrists and lower arms are great to prevent burning.
PARCHMENT PAPER & FOIL	Parchment paper is essential for baking and for baking vegetables with no added oil. It is good for temperatures up to 450°F (232°C). Foil is great for covering foods as they bake so they do not dry out or to cover the inside of pans to cut clean up.
SCALE	Helps in accuracy and speed in baking and other cooking. They are inexpensive.
SERVING SPOONS and SLOTTED SPOONS	For stirring and moving contents in pots or pans.
SLOW COOKER OR CROCKPOT	For batch cooking on a weekend or to leave food available for children when they come home from school, it's a lifesaver. You can make soups, chili and so much more.
SPATULAS	High-temperature plastic, metal or wooden spatulas are essential for all sorts of cooking. Buy several. You will use lots of them.
STAINLESS STEEL POTS and PANS	A good assortment of pans is essential, and these will be used every day. A steamer insert is also a good addition for steaming instead of boiling, which retains nutrients in vegetables.
TAPE or LABELS	Great for marking what is in a container. The date is also helpful for leftovers, which cuts food waste and cost.
TONGS	Tongs in various sizes are essential for moving foods in and out of the oven or on a grill.
ZESTER	This is an inexpensive tool that started as a rasp for wood working but is now essential in the kitchen. It allows you to zest any citrus fruit you use. The peel is where a lot of the nutrition is, so don't throw it away. It only takes a minute to zest a lemon.

Stocking Your Pantry

For your personal food preferences, your kitchen pantry can be stocked to make cooking and baking more efficient. Where organic versions are available, I choose them as they are non-GMO. Many of these items are used in the recipes in the book, so they are listed here. Stock those that appeal to you until you know what your go-to foods, spices and herbs will be.

STAPLES:

ARROWROOT STARCH	This is a starch that is used in place of cornstarch as a tasteless thickener.
BEANS, LEGUMES and CHICKPEAS	These are inexpensive pantry items that can be used to make meals or dips, such as hummus. Dried beans and legumes are less expensive but must be soaked. Canned versions with BPA-free packaging are a good alternative.
CAROB	It can be used as a chocolate substitute and has nutrition benefits such as calcium, potassium, caffeine-free and oxalate-free.
DIJON or STONE GROUND MUSTARD & MUSTARD SEED	Essential for that French mellow, yet sharp mustard taste with a spicy finish. Mustard seed adds a tart flavour and is part of a cheese flavour in plant-based sauces.
FLAXSEED	This high-value grain is great for heart health and can be combined with water to substitute for eggs.
FLOUR	In addition to all purpose flour, consider almond, buckwheat, rice, rye, tapioca, whole wheat and whole wheat pastry flour.
GARLIC	This allium is healthy and adds flavour to everything. I buy fresh garlic and peel it by hand.
MACA ROOT POWDER	Used by the Incas, it has qualities that improve sexual vitality. There is red maca for women and black maca for men. Maca root has a positive effect not only on sexual organs but also on the whole endocrine system. It can be found in most health food stores. themacateam.com is also a great source.
MONK FRUIT (PURE)	This is my preference to sweeten many baked goods since it has no calories. It is 300 times sweeter than sugar. It has been used for thousands of years in Asia and is on the FDA GRAS (Generally Recognized as Safe) list. There are products that are mainly erythritol (which is a sugar alcohol), mixed with some monk fruit. These are not pure monk fruit and are not recommended.
NUT and SEED BUTTERS	These can often be used in place of regular butter. Almond, walnut, peanut cashew, sunflower seed and pumpkin seed butters containing no added oils, sugar or salt are all healthy, high in protein and have no cholesterol.
NUTRITIONAL YEAST	Not to be confused with traditional yeast, this has large yellow flakes and is high in B vitamins. It's a great stand-in for cheese in many dishes.

NUTS	Almonds, walnuts, cashews, hazelnuts, pistachios and more are excellent for snacks and a great addition to many baked goods and salads.
OATS	Rolled oats and steel cut oats are great for breakast. Rolled oats can be used for baking and are gluten-free.
ONIONS	Essential to flavours for so many dishes and makes sautéing without oil much easier.
PLANT-BASED MILKS	Almond, soy or oat milks are great alternatives to dairy milk. They are lower in calories and saturated fats and have no cholesterol. Today's plant-based milks are also enriched with vitamins and minerals, such as vitamin D and calcium. Some brands include vanilla, which I think adds sweetness without sugar or extra calories.
SALT	Sea salt should have colour, which shows that it still has mineral content and has not been baked at extremely high temperatures. Black salt (Himalyan) is used to emulate an egg flavour in some plant-based sauces.
SESAME SEEDS and OTHER SEEDS	These add flavour and beauty to many dishes and salads. Other examples would be pumpkin seeds, sunflower seeds, caraway seeds and fennel seeds.
STRAINED TOMATOES	Canned or bottled tomatoes are good for using in cooking. It's best to avoid those with many additives such as salt. Strained tomatoes, called passata, are excellent when you do not want seeds or skins in a dish.
SWEET POTATOES and POTATOES	These are inexpensive and keep a long time. A great item to have available for emergency meals. Nutritious, low-calorie and a source of good carbs.
TAMARI	Similar to soy sauce but with other benefits but it has no wheat. It contains niacin (vitamin B3), manganese, protein, and tryptophan. Be sure to get a brand that does not have *added* salt.
TOFU	Tofu is high in protein and can be used as an egg substitute and in place of dairy in alternative mayonnaise recipes. It comes in soft, all the way to extra firm. It is frequently enriched with calcium.

SPICES AND HERBS:

ALMOND EXTRACT	Helpful for that extra kick in sweet crusts and baked goods.
ANISE SEEDS	Add sweetness to many dishes. They can be ground as well.
BASIL	Sweet basil, fresh or dried, is great for many dishes.
CHILLI POWDER and RED PEPPER FLAKES	Adds spice to many dishes. Other great peppers are harissa, chipotle, cayenne or hot Thai peppers.
CINNAMON	Ceylon cinnamon is the mildest and very aromatic. Vietnamese cinnamon is aromatic and a bit hot. Madagascar cinnamon is pungent and great tasting. All are perfect for baked goods and adding sweetness without sugar.
CURRY POWDER	Both red and yellow – adds heat and complex flavours to savoury dishes.
FENUGREEK	Tastes a little like maple syrup and adds a sweet taste to dishes.

FRENCH TARRAGON	A lovely aromatic herb that adds a licorice-like taste in savoury dishes.
GARLIC POWDER	Good to have as many recipes call for it, and it is less hot than raw garlic.
GROUND CARDAMOM	Strong-tasting, so a little goes a long way. It adds a great aromatic, exotic dimension to fruit pies and more.
GROUND CORIANDER	A sweeter-tasting herb that can be added for complexity in a variety of dishes.
GROUND CUMIN	Adds a familiar beefy taste in many dishes such as chili, promotes digestion and cuts inflammation.
GINGER	Wonderful fresh or ground for adding heat flavour to sweet or savoury dishes.
MACE or NUTMEG	Mace is the spicier part of the fruit of the tree that both nutmeg and mace come from. Both add earthy nutty flavour and sweetness without sugar.
MARJORAM	Often overlooked, but this herb has a great aroma and citrusy, floral taste that adds complexity to many dishes.
MINT	Mint can be added to drinks and dishes to add a sweet, aromatic dimension.
ONION POWDER	A great substitute for fresh onions and in many plant-based cheeses.
OREGANO	Fresh or dried, this herb is pungent, earthy, strong and aromatic.
ROSEMARY	Beautiful to decorate with, it also adds a distinctive lemon-pine flavour.
SAGE	A great herb for tomato dishes or veggie burgers with its earthy, minty and citrusy flavours.
SMOKED PAPRIKA	This spice perks up many dishes with its smoky aroma and hot pepper notes.
THYME	A great aromatic herb that can be added to many dishes.
TURMERIC	This spice adds colour and health to every dish and adds powerful anti-inflammatory benefits too.
VANILLA EXTRACT	Adds a warm sweetness to foods and baked goods. Buy genuine vanilla extract, not imitation.

FLAVOUR WITH BENEFITS

Great tasting food and wonderful flavours are some of the consistent joys in life. We believe there should be no compromise on flavour or nutrition. Because of this, the ingredients in the recipes have been selected to meet both criteria. In our experience, this allows us to make healthy changes in our food choices and sustain these changes.

This chapter is a primer on the role of foods we consume and their impacts on health, and the role of nutrition and lifestyle in improving our overall well-being. References to scientific studies are provided to substantiate the reasons for statements made in the book and the recipe ingredients and cooking methods selected.

These sections are:

- Flavour and Food Preferences
- Food as Medicine
- Ingredient Substitutions for Healthier Outcomes
- Our Food Journey
- North American Nutrition Guidance
- Nutrition Categories:
    - Macronutrients
    - Micronutrients
- Consideration of Dietary Options
- Impacts of Food Choices and Exercise

FLAVOUR AND FOOD PREFERENCES

Flavour and palatability influence what people consume.[1] Babies form some of their food and sweetness preferences before they are born and these are largely set by the time they are five years old. This makes early food choices crucial for children's health.[2]

The topic of food and flavours became such a passion that I invested in some courses to learn more about nutrition and its impact on our overall health. What I learned surprised me about food as medicine. But it shouldn't have been a surprise. We eat several times a day, so why wouldn't food be fundamental to our overall health. What if some "facts" we believed were not completely true? What if the answers to good health were not complex at all but quite simple?

---

[1]   Pandurangan M, Hwang I. Systemic mechanism of taste, flavour and palatability in brain. Appl Biochem Biotechnol. 2015
[2]   Murray R, D: Savoring Sweet: Sugars in Infant and Toddler Feeding. Ann Nutr Metab 2017;70(suppl 3):38-46. doi: 10.1159/000479246

FOOD AS MEDICINE

As I thought about this, I remembered what I learned at five years old about a food remedy with artichokes to cleanse my liver. Our bodies already know how to detect and manage toxins and nutrients in food, without intervention. I knew from my early experience that eating nutritious foods promotes health and can heal us. What if our food was the answer to preventing seven out of ten of the top fatal diseases in North America?

What if heart disease, osteoporosis, cancer, high blood pressure and dementia, are directly related to what we eat? What if conditions such as erectile dysfunction are a sign that arteries are already clogged? Traditional western medicine seems content to monitor our decline in health and prescribe pills to manage symptoms.

Since 1-2% of health conditions are congenital, then there must be other causes for our decline in health. If 90% of men, and an equally alarming percentage of women, at age 65 are diagnosed with heart disease in North America, isn't this an epidemic?

After more research, I became convinced that some of my own current health issues could be solved by dietary changes. Pills had unwanted side effects. It might take time, but it was worth a try.

INGREDIENT SUBSTITUTIONS FOR HEALTHIER OUTCOMES

In late 2019, I began making substitutions to lower fat in some recipes, such as replacing cream with yoghurt. This reduced the saturated fats and lowered the calories. Not being a refined sugar fan, I explored other sweetener options. I started using stevia, a natural sweetener which is readily available in grocery stores. It was good for calorie reduction but for me, it did not meet the flavour requirement. So I pressed on. I stumbled on monk fruit, which is grown in China and Thailand and has been a natural sweetener in use for thousands of years. Another option was Yacon root from South America. It has a pleasant caramel flavour, but availability can be an issue.

I settled on monk fruit which is about 300 times sweeter than sugar and organic sources are available in stores or online. This replacement was not without its early failures in baking, because it cannot be substituted one for one with sugar. After many attempts and failures, the monk fruit measurements in the recipes, work both for a level of sweetness and for a difference in volume when replacing sugar.

Next was cheese. That is a big one. Yes. Humans are the only species that consume milk from another mammal. Cow, sheep or goat's milk are great for their babies, but not for humans. Thus, we may have health side effects from consuming milk. This is discussed in more detail later in this section.

Because cheese is such a fundamental favourite and flavour, it was a bigger task to replace. Having been a long-time fan of baking sourdough bread and being familiar with some health benefits of fermented foods, I thought why not look into plant-based cheeses some that were fermented and those that were not. There are many sources of plant-based cheeses in stores or we have a few recipes for you to try. Plant-based cheeses are made often with nuts, nutritional yeast, garlic powder and onion powder. Some "cheese" sauces use vegetables such as potatoes for texture along with other flavours to provide a cheese-like taste.

Another important flavour challenge was the beefy or umami flavour that is central to many dishes. It became clear that sautéing various types of mushrooms with onions and garlic was a great start. Adding spices and herbs such as cumin, smoked paprika, tamari, onions and garlic yielded familiar meaty aromas and flavours.

The last area was a bit more challenging. It involved cooking and baking without extracted oil. An ingredient that has 100% of its calories from fat, is just not healthy, no matter what it's made from. Turns out extracted oil is a big contributor to heart disease. It forms plaque in the arteries and kills off some cells that are critical to blood flow.

So how to cook and bake without oil was a bit disorienting, since every recipe I had been using had oil as an ingredient. I found that starting with a hot pan, especially a cast-iron skillet and adding a bit of water or tamari, allowed me to sauté many vegetables including onions and garlic. Not too difficult after a few tries. What a difference this made on calories and fat.

OUR FOOD JOURNEY

This path may not be for everyone. But it has worked for me and my husband. At first, he was not convinced, but he had some health goals and thought, the only thing he might have to lose, was weight! He started making his versions of our favourite foods: tasty salads and soups. We learned that if you eat soup prior to a meal, you may consume about 20% fewer calories for your total meal.

Let's face it, no one wants to be lectured about what they should or should not eat. We know from our own experience that major food changes may be difficult and take time, so we have included recipes in the book for everyone. Some are plant-based recipes, others include dairy, chicken, fish and steak. We have now chosen to embrace a 90% plant-based diet and have seen our health improve.

We actually both lost weight, my husband's blood pressure declined and our cholesterol levels went from dangerous to excellent. Our doctor was pleased with the results and said, "whatever you are doing, keep doing it".

What we learned: overall health impacts everything, even our sexual health. Indications such as low energy or heart palpitations are early warning signs that some changes to diet are needed. Diet trumps everything and either helps or hurts our general health. Make some small changes and receive big benefits in your health.

We also combined our food changes with consistent vigorous exercise to continue to augment our dietary changes. Long walks have become the norm. That fresh air is good for the body and soul. This is our experience and it worked for us. Your experience may be different, but the best thing is to start today. The return on your food investment may surprise you.

Now on to the details and scientific references that support food as medicine.

NORTH AMERICAN NUTRITION GUIDANCE

CANADIAN GOVERNMENT GUIDANCE

The Canada Food Guide, which was revamped and published in January 2019, encourages the following: eat plenty of vegetables and fruits, whole grain foods and choose protein foods from plants more often; limit highly processed foods, make water your drink of choice, read food labels, cook more often at home and beware of food marketing that can influence your food choices.[3]

AMERICAN MEDICAL ASSOCIATION (AMA) REQUEST TO US DEPARTMENT OF AGRICULTURE

In a letter dated Aug. 13, 2020, the AMA wrote: "The AMA supports culturally responsive dietary and nutritional guidelines and recognizes that racial and ethnic disparities exist in the prevalence of obesity and diet-related diseases such as coronary heart disease, cancer, stroke, and diabetes. Dairy and meat products are promoted in federal nutrition policies even though they are not nutritionally required..."[4]

NUTRITION CATEGORIES

CARBOHYDRATES

Good carbohydrates are one macronutrient that is essential to health. They should be 45– 65% of your diet, or 900 to 1,300 calories out of a 2,000-calorie allowance. The type of carbohydrate matters. Whole grains (i.e. oats and whole wheat bread), beans (pulses and legumes), potatoes, sweet potatoes and brown rice, for example, have healthy carbohydrates as well as other benefits such as high fibre.[5]

Net carbohydrates are calculated on a food label: as carbohydrates per serving, less the fibre equals the digestible carbs or net carbs.[6] High-fibre content means fewer of the calories will be absorbed. Food labels in several countries are being revamped to include more information as well as more realistic portion sizes so that intelligent food decisions are easier to make.

PROTEIN

Protein is an essential macronutrient, but excess protein is stored as fat and can cause weight gain. Recommendations vary, but 46 grams per day is the guideline for a sedentary woman.[7]

Most Americans eat twice as much protein as they need.[8] A steak that weighs 100 grams has 25 grams of protein, over half of what is recommended for a sedentary woman for one day.

FAT AND SATURATED FATS

Fat is also a macronutrient, and it is necessary for life. No more than 10% of daily calories should come from saturated fats.[9]

In the North American diet, 33% of calories come from fat and 13% from saturated fats. Between 180 and 320 milligrams per day of cholesterol are consumed. Major sources of saturated fats are animal sources, including milk, pastries, cheese, margarine and mayonnaise.[10]

All oil is high in fat. Olive oil is 120 calories per tablespoon, 100% from fat. The beneficial part of olive oil is the polyphenols and plant sterols. These only occur in extra virgin olive oil. But all plants have polyphenols

---

[3] https://food-guide.canada.ca/en/healthy-food-choices/, January 2019.
[4] https://www.pcrm.org/news/blog/american-medical-association-calls-dietary-guidelines-indicate-meat-and-dairy-products
[5] https://www.mayoclinic.org/healthy-lifestyle/nutrition-and-healthy-eating/in-depth/carbohydrates/art-20045705https
[6] https://dtc.ucsf.edu/living-with-diabetes/diet-and-nutrition/understanding-carbohydrates/counting-carbohydrates/learning-to-read-labels/understanding-fiber/
[7] https://www.healthline.com/nutrition/how-much-protein-per-day
[8] https://newsnetwork.mayoclinic.org/discussion/are-you-getting-too-much-protein/
[9] https://medlineplus.gov/ency/patientinstructions/000838.htm
[10] Esperanza J Carcache de Blanco & Jay Mirtallo, Nutrition: An Approach to Good Health and Disease Management, Bentham Books, 2015, p. 92.

and plant sterols, and eating the plants (such as olives) provides the benefits without the high-fat content of extracted oils. High-fat content in your diet leads to weight gain and cardiovascular disease.[11]

The Diabetes Association food guide recommends a low-carb, low-salt and low-fat diet to cut the risk of diabetes.[12]

VITAMINS AND MINERALS

Eating a rainbow of plants will provide a wide variety of vitamins and minerals without the need for as many supplements.[13] [14]

Plant-based sources of calcium are plentiful and have no cholesterol. They are either low in or have zero saturated fats, making them a great alternative to dairy. Calcium, an essential mineral, is needed for bone growth, muscles, heart health and nerve health.[15]

Nutritional yeast is a great source of B vitamins, including B12, which is less prevalent naturally in a plant-based diet.[16]

CHOLESTEROL

The human body makes all the cholesterol it needs.[17] Other sources of cholesterol are from meat, dairy and eggs. Plants do not have any cholesterol and, therefore, do not increase your cholesterol levels. High cholesterol levels cause plaque in arteries and lead to cardiovascular disease.

In the US, inherited or familial high cholesterol occurs in 1 in 250 people or 0.4%.[18] For most of us, what we eat is contributing to our cholesterol levels. Adding more plant-based foods to your diet can help manage cholesterol levels.[19]

Cheddar cheese (compared to the cashew cheese recipe presented in this book) has about twice as many calories as the plant-based option. Of the 115 total calories for an ounce of cheddar, 85 come from fat versus 43 calories from fat for the cashew cheese. Cholesterol from cheddar cheese is 28 milligrams compared to zero for the cashew cheese.

Cream cheese has 102 calories per serving of 2 tablespoons, 29 milligrams of cholesterol and 90% of the calories from fat.[20] Vegan cream cheese (from Kite Hill, for example), by contrast, has 70 calories per 2 tablespoons, zero cholesterol and 60% of calories from fat.[21]

DIETARY FIBRE

Only plants have fibre. The recommended daily fibre intake for women ranges from 21 to 25 grams. The average American gets 15 grams.[22]

High-fibre diets and healthy gut bacteria are essential to a reduction in disease. The gastrointestinal microbiota have an important role in human health, and there is increasing interest in utilizing dietary approaches to modulate the composition and metabolic function of the microbial communities that colonise

[11] https://www.pritikin.com/your-health/healthy-living/eating-right/1103-whats-wrong-with-olive-oil.html
[12] https://www.diabetescarecommunity.ca/diet-and-fitness-articles/diabetes-diet-articles/healthy-meal-preparation/
[13] https://foodrevolution.org/blog/eating-the-rainbow-health-benefits/
[14] https://www.hindawi.com/journals/jnme/2019/2125070/
[15] https://www.mayoclinic.org/healthy-lifestyle/nutrition-and-healthy-eating/in-depth/calcium-supplements/art-20047097
[16] https://www.medicalnewstoday.com/articles/323245
[17] https://www.hopkinsmedicine.org/health/conditions-and-diseases/high-cholesterol/cholesterol-in-the-blood
[18] https://www.heart.org/en/health-topics/cholesterol/causes-of-high-cholesterol/familial-hypercholesterolemia-fh
[19] Jakše, B., Jakše, B., Pajek, J., & Pajek, M. (2019). Effects of ad libitum consumed, low-fat, high-fiber plant-based diet supplemented with plant-based meal replacements on cardiovascular risk factors. Food & Nutrition Research, 63. https://doi.org/10.29219/fnr.v63.1560
[20] https://www.nutritionix.com/food/cream-cheese
[21] https://www.kite-hill.com/our-food/cream-cheese-style-spreads/
[22] https://www.healthline.com/health/food-nutrition/how-much-fiber-per-day

the gastrointestinal tract to improve health and prevent or treat disease. One dietary strategy for modulating the microbiota is consumption of dietary fibre and prebiotics that can be metabolized by microbes in the gastrointestinal tract.[23]

High-fibre foods are nutrient-dense and low in calorie density.[24] This means that with high-fibre plant-based foods, you can generally eat as much as you want without gaining weight.

CONSIDERATION OF DIETARY OPTIONS

DAIRY

After infancy, 65% of the human population is lactose intolerant. It is most prevalent in East Asians where it ranges from 70 to 100% and common among people of West African, Arab, Jewish, Greek and Italian descent. Only 5% of Northern Europeans are lactose intolerant.[25] Cow's milk is not a good fit for most human children and adults. This would include all dairy, such as liquid milk, cream and cheese.

Milk is not part of a low-fat diet. Whole milk has approximately 150 calories, 71 of which come from fat.[26] Even 2%-fat milk gets a third of its calories from fat.[27]

Yoghurt vs. cream cheese.[28] Regular cream cheese has 350 calories per 100 grams and 34 grams of fat (or 34% fat). Plain full-fat yoghurt has 107 calories and 6 grams of fat.

Yoghurt[29][30] is abundant in calcium, zinc, B vitamins, and probiotics; it is a good source of protein; and it may be supplemented with vitamin D and additional probiotics associated with positive health outcomes.[31] Nondairy yoghurt also is abundant with probiotics and is a good alternative for people who want to avoid dairy.

SOY AND FERMENTED SOY PRODUCTS

Soybeans, tofu, tempeh and miso are soy products that contribute health benefits such as lowering breast cancer risk, reducing hot flashes and reducing stress on kidneys, compared to eating animal protein.[32] Many soy products also contain high levels of calcium. Consumption of soy became controversial for two reasons: 1.) Some nonorganic soybeans are genetically modified to be more resistant to pesticides using a genetic modification, creating Bt Toxins which are harmful to humans.[33] Choose organic soy products to avoid this. 2.) Soybean isolates appear to have negative results only when daily servings exceed five to seven servings a day.[34]

[23] Holscher HD. Dietary fiber and prebiotics and the gastrointestinal microbiota. Gut Microbes. 2017 Mar 4;8(2):172-184. doi: 10.1080/19490976.2017.1290756. Epub 2017 Feb 6. PMID: 28165863; PMCID: PMC5390821

[24] https://www.webmd.com/cholesterol-management/features/fiber-groceries

[25] https://ghr.nlm.nih.gov/condition/lactose-intolerance#statistics

[26] https://www.nutritionix.com/food/whole-milk

[27] https://www.nutritionix.com/food/milk

[28] https://fdc.nal.usda.gov/fdc-app.html#/food-details/173418/nutrients

[29] El-Abbadi NH, Dao MC, Meydani SN. Yogurt: role in healthy and active aging. Am J Clin Nutr. 2014 May;99(5 Suppl):1263S-70S. doi: 10.3945/ajcn.113.073957. Epub 2014 Apr 2. PMID: 24695886; PMCID: PMC6410895

[30] https://www.nbcnews.com/better/health/10-smart-swaps-will-save-you-hundreds-calories-ncna828706

[31] El-Abbadi NH, Dao MC, Meydani SN. Yogurt: role in healthy and active aging. Am J Clin Nutr. 2014;99(5 Suppl):1263S-70S. doi:10.3945/ajcn.113.073957

[32] https://nutritionfacts.org/video/should-women-at-high-risk-for-breast-cancer-avoid-soy/

[33] National Academies of Sciences, Engineering, and Medicine; Division on Earth and Life Studies; Board on Agriculture and Natural Resources; Committee on Genetically Engineered Crops: Past Experience and Future Prospects. Genetically Engineered Crops: Experiences and Prospects. Washington (DC): National Academies Press (US); 2016 May 17. 5, Human Health Effects of Genetically Engineered Crops. Available from: https://www.ncbi.nlm.nih.gov/books/NBK424534/

[34] https://nutritionfacts.org/video/how-much-soy-is-too-much/

SUGAR

Sugar is one of the most addictive substances on earth. Biologically, we are wired to prefer sweeter foods to others, due to our need for glucose for energy. But refined sugars are one of the most inflammatory substances we can consume, compared to the natural sweetness of fruits. Sugar intake also has an impact on cancers, such as breast cancer.[35]

Much of the sugar added to processed foods is high-fructose syrup, which can lead to a higher risk of obesity and insulin resistance.[36]

Fructose-sweetened drinks contribute to high blood pressure by increasing uric acid, which decreases the synthesis of nitric oxide. This, in turn, inhibits vascular smooth muscle relaxant.[37]

High consumption of sugar and sugary beverages increases cancer risk.[38] Lower consumption of sugar leads to a higher intake of fibre and better health outcomes.[39]

NATURAL SWEETENERS

Monk fruit is a natural sweetener that has been used for thousands of years. It is on the FDA GRAS (Generally Recognized As Safe) list.[40] It has no calories and may help with weight management in place of sugar. One study has shown the antioxidant effects of monk fruit.[41] Some studies group monk fruit and stevia together with sucralose and aspartame and classify them as nonnutritive sweeteners. Monk fruit and stevia are directly derived from plants, just like maple syrup.[42][43][44]

Pure monk fruit is superior to monk fruit mixed with erythritol. Erythritol is a sugar alcohol. It has been known to lead to abdominal discomfort and diarrhea,[45] and for those who have chronic Irritable Bowel Syndrome (IBS), it may irritate it further.[46]

CAROB

Using carob in addition to cocoa powder in "chocolate" foods can help lower cholesterol[47] and improve anti-cancer activity by 36%.[48] It also has genisteins, which have anti-tumour properties.[49]

[35] Jiang Y, Pan Y, Rhea PR, Tan L, Gagea M, Cohen L, Fischer SM, Yang P. A Sucrose-Enriched Diet Promotes Tumorigenesis in Mammary Gland in Part through the 12-Lipoxygenase Pathway. Cancer Res. 2016 Jan 1;76(1):24-9. doi: 10.1158/0008-5472.CAN-14-3432. PMID: 26729790; PMCID: PMC4703949.

[36] Bray GA, Nielsen SJ, Popkin BM. Consumption of high-fructose corn syrup in beverages may play a role in the epidemic of obesity. Am J Clin Nutr. 2004 Apr;79(4):537-43. doi: 10.1093/ajcn/79.4.537. Erratum in: Am J Clin Nutr. 2004 Oct;80(4):1090. PMID: 15051594.

[37] https://www.tandfonline.com/doi/full/10.1586/erc.10.120

[38] Consumption of Sugars, Sugary Foods, and Sugary Beverages in Relation to Adiposity-Related Cancer Risk in the Framingham Offspring Cohort (1991–2013),Nour Makarem, Elisa V. Bandera, Yong Lin, Paul F. Jacques, Richard B. Hayes and Niyati Parekh, Cancer Prev Res June 1 2018 (11) (6) 347-358; DOI: 10.1158/1940-6207.CAPR-17-0218

[39] Wang YF, Chiavaroli L, Roke K, DiAngelo C, Marsden S, Sievenpiper J. Canadian Adults with Moderate Intakes of Total Sugars have Greater Intakes of Fibre and Key Micronutrients: Results from the Canadian Community Health Survey 2015 Public Use Microdata File. Nutrients. 2020;12(4):1124. Published 2020 Apr 17. doi:10.3390/nu12041124

[40] https://www.fda.gov/food/food-additives-petitions/additional-information-about-high-intensity-sweeteners-permitted-use-food-united-states

[41] W. J. Chen, J. Wang, X. Y. Qi & B. J. Xie (2007) The antioxidant activities of natural sweeteners, mogrosides, from fruits of Siraitia grosvenori, International Journal of Food Sciences and Nutrition, 58:7, 548-556, DOI: 10.1080/09637480701336360

[42] Anti-inflammatory Activities of Mogrosides from Momordica grosvenori in Murine Macrophages and a Murine Ear Edema Model,Rong Di, Mou-Tuan Huang, and Chi-Tang Ho,Journal of Agricultural and Food Chemistry 2011 59 (13), 7474-7481,DOI: 10.1021/jf201207m

[43] Pepino MY. Metabolic effects of non-nutritive sweeteners. Physiol Behav. 2015;152(Pt B):450-455. doi:10.1016/j.physbeh.2015.06.024

[44] Ahmad SY, Azad MB, Friel J, MacKay D. Recent evidence for the effects of nonnutritive sweeteners on glycaemic control. Curr Opin Clin Nutr Metab Care. 2019 Jul;22(4):278-283. doi: 10.1097/MCO.0000000000000566. PMID: 31033578

[45] Lenhart A, Chey WD. A Systematic Review of the Effects of Polyols on Gastrointestinal Health and Irritable Bowel Syndrome. Adv Nutr. 2017;8(4):587-596. Published 2017 Jul 14. doi:10.3945/an.117.015560

[46] https://www.healthline.com/nutrition/sugar-alcohols-good-or-bad#section6

[47] https://my.clevelandclinic.org/health/articles/17368-phytosterols-sterols--stanols

[48] Pawłowska K, Kuligowski M, Jasińska-Kuligowska I, et al. Effect of Replacing Cocoa Powder by Carob Powder in the Muffins on Sensory and Physicochemical Properties. Plant Foods Hum Nutr. 2018;73(3):196-202. doi:10.1007/s11130-018-0675-0

[49] https://www.merriam-webster.com/dictionary/genistein

FOODS WITH ANTIOXIDANTS

Various varieties of blueberries contain high levels of antioxidants.[50] Antioxidants are molecules that fight free radicals in your body. Free radicals are compounds that cause harm if their levels become too high and are linked to illnesses including diabetes, heart disease, and cancer.[51]

Citrus flavonoids are antioxidants with benefits. They help strengthen cell walls, blood vessels and lymph systems and reduce cholesterol.[52]

Fermented foods such as sourdough bread, assist in digestion and degrade phytates, which means that the absorption of minerals is increased and insulin spikes are reduced.[53]

MACA ROOT

Sun-dried and traditionally dried Maca (red, yellow and black) aid in sexual vitality, higher energy, higher sperm count (black maca) and better bone health.[54][55] About two thousand years ago, the Incas developed and grew maca root to improve the health, energy and sexual well-being of their citizens.

The harvest and drying methods are important to the end quality of the powder. This is why choosing a good source is very important. Themacateam.com is a credible source to consider.

IMPACTS OF FOOD CHOICES AND EXERCISE

INFLAMMATION AND DISEASE

Plant-based diets assist in healthier gut bacteria and reduce inflammation caused by food.[56] Unchecked chronic inflammation is now thought to be responsible for many cancers and deadly cardiovascular diseases, including atherosclerosis and painful arthritis.[57]

Flaxseed has many health benefits, including anti-inflammatory properties.[58] Regular consumption of ground flaxseed can reduce inflammation and has been shown to reduce menopausal symptoms. In the eighth century, King Charlemagne passed a law that required his subjects to eat flaxseed due to its health benefits.[59]

Turmeric has been used for thousands of years and has anti-inflammatory properties.[60] It is proven effective in reducing the symptoms of arthritis,[61] and it is readily available and affordable to add spice and yellow colour to food. No need to buy it as a supplement.

---

[50] Kim JG, Kim HL, Kim SJ, Park KS. Fruit quality, anthocyanin and total phenolic contents, and antioxidant activities of 45 blueberry cultivars grown in Suwon, Korea. J Zhejiang Univ Sci B. 2013;14(9):793-799. doi:10.1631/jzus.B1300012

[51] https://www.healthline.com/nutrition/antioxidants-explained

[52] https://www.winchesterhospital.org/health-library/article?id=21574

[53] https://www.healthline.com/nutrition/sourdough-bread#section6

[54] Gonzales GF. Ethnobiology and Ethnopharmacology of Lepidium meyenii (Maca), a Plant from the Peruvian Highlands. Evid Based Complement Alternat Med. 2012;2012:193496. doi:10.1155/2012/193496

[55] Gonzales GF, Gonzales C, Gonzales-Castañeda C. Lepidium meyenii (Maca): a plant from the highlands of Peru--from tradition to science. Forsch Komplementmed. 2009 Dec;16(6):373-80. doi: 10.1159/000242618. Epub 2009 Dec 16. PMID: 20090350.

[56] Glick-Bauer M, Yeh MC. The health advantage of a vegan diet: exploring the gut microbiota connection. Nutrients. 2014;6(11):4822-4838. Published 2014 Oct 31. doi:10.3390/nu6114822

[57] Wiejak J, Dunlop J, Mackay SP, Yarwood SJ. Flavanoids induce expression of the suppressor of cytokine signalling 3 (SOCS3) gene and suppress IL-6-activated signal transducer and activator of transcription 3 (STAT3) activation in vascular endothelial cells. Biochem J. 2013;454(2):283-293. doi:10.1042/BJ20130481

[58] Parikh M, Maddaford TG, Austria JA, Aliani M, Netticadan T, Pierce GN. Dietary Flaxseed as a Strategy for Improving Human Health. Nutrients. 2019;11(5):1171. Published 2019 May 25. doi:10.3390/nu11051171

[59] https://www.canr.msu.edu/news/flaxseed_is_it_the_new_superfood

[60] https://www.canr.msu.edu/news/health_benefits_of_turmeric

[61] Daily JW, Yang M, Park S. Efficacy of Turmeric Extracts and Curcumin for Alleviating the Symptoms of Joint Arthritis: A Systematic Review and Meta-Analysis of Randomized Clinical Trials. J Med Food. 2016;19(8):717-729. doi:10.1089/jmf.2016.3705

HEART HEALTH

Cruciferous vegetables and leafy greens are crucial for heart health, due to their levels of nitric oxide. Nitric oxide is involved in many physiological and pathological processes, such as relaxing vascular smooth muscle tissue, increasing regional blood flow and inhibiting platelet and leukocyte adhesion to vessel walls. A combination of all these physiological benefits is likely to slow the progression of atherosclerosis.[62][63]

The oils and saturated fats added to food damage the endothelial cells, which is one cause of heart disease. Eliminating added oils, of any type, from cooked and baked foods helps reduce and even reverse this damage.[64]

HIGH BLOOD PRESSURE MANAGEMENT

Hibiscus may have cancer-fighting properties and helps with natural reduction of hypertension.[65][66][67] High fibre, plant-based diets lead to better weight management and may enable people to lower their blood pressure naturally.[68]

LIVER HEALTH

For liver health, green leafy vegetables can modulate liver fatty acid composition, thus providing protection against elevations in atherogenic fatty acids, those that promote fatty plaque in the arteries.[69] This is an easy way to improve liver health.

Long-term dietary supplementation with artichoke extract significantly improves blood lipid profile. Antioxidants contained in artichokes can also protect the liver from the harmful effects of toxins and heavy metals. This plant is a member of the thistle family. Due to their rich basic composition and high levels of antioxidants, artichokes can likely be used in the prevention of chronic noncommunicable diseases, namely those resulting from oxidative damage.[70]

TYPE 2 DIABETES PREVENTION

Over half a billion people have type 2 diabetes.[71] A wholefood plant-based diet has been shown to prevent or treat diabetes.[72] It is an easy lifestyle to follow because you don't have to count calories and limit your portions.[73] Compared to nonvegetarians, clinical trials have shown a lower rate of type 2 diabetes.[74]

[62] Blekkenhorst LC, Sim M, Bondonno CP, et al. Cardiovascular Health Benefits of Specific Vegetable Types: A Narrative Review. Nutrients. 2018;10(5):595. Published 2018 May 11. doi:10.3390/nu10050595

[63] Blekkenhorst LC, Bondonno CP, Lewis JR, et al. Cruciferous and Allium Vegetable Intakes are Inversely Associated With 15-Year Atherosclerotic Vascular Disease Deaths in Older Adult Women. J Am Heart Assoc. 2017;6(10):e006558. Published 2017 Oct 24. doi:10.1161/JAHA.117.006558

[64] https://www.dresselstyn.com/huffpost.htm

[65] Hopkins AL, Lamm MG, Funk JL, Ritenbaugh C. Hibiscus sabdariffa L. in the treatment of hypertension and hyperlipidemia: a comprehensive review of animal and human studies. Fitoterapia. 2013;85:84-94. doi:10.1016/j.fitote.2013.01.003

[66] Nguyen, C., Baskaran, K., Pupulin, A. et al. Hibiscus flower extract selectively induces apoptosis in breast cancer cells and positively interacts with common chemotherapeutics. BMC Complement Altern Med 19, 98 (2019). https://doi.org/10.1186/s12906-019-2505-9

[67] Abubakar SM, Ukeyima MT, Spencer JPE, Lovegrove JA. Acute Effects of Hibiscus Sabdariffa Calyces on Postprandial Blood Pressure, Vascular Function, Blood Lipids, Biomarkers of Insulin Resistance and Inflammation in Humans. Nutrients. 2019;11(2):341. Published 2019 Feb 5. doi:10.3390/nu11020341

[68] Semlitsch T, Jeitler K, Berghold A, et al. Long-term effects of weight-reducing diets in people with hypertension. Cochrane Database Syst Rev. 2016;3(3):CD008274. Published 2016 Mar 2. doi:10.1002/14651858.CD008274.pub3

[69] Johnson M, Pace RD, Dawkins NL, Willian KR. Diets containing traditional and novel green leafy vegetables improve liver fatty acid profiles of spontaneously hypertensive rats. Lipids Health Dis. 2013;12:168. Published 2013 Nov 5. doi:10.1186/1476-511X-12-168

[70] Biel W, Witkowicz R, Piątkowska E, Podsiadło C. Proximate Composition, Minerals and Antioxidant Activity of Artichoke Leaf Extracts. Biol Trace Elem Res. 2020;194(2):589-595. doi:10.1007/s12011-019-01806-3

[71] Diabetes 2018 Jul; 67(Supplement 1): -.https://doi.org/10.2337/db18-202-LB

[72] McMacken M, Shah S. A plant-based diet for the prevention and treatment of type 2 diabetes. J Geriatr Cardiol. 2017;14(5):342-354. doi:10.11909/j.issn.1671-5411.2017.05.009

[73] https://www.pcrm.org/health-topics/diabetes

[74] Preparing to Prescribe Plant-Based Diets for Diabetes Prevention and Treatment, Caroline Trapp, MSN, APRN, BC-ADM,   CDE and Susan Levin, MS, RD, Diabetes Spectrum 2012 Feb; 25(1): 38-44.https://doi.org/10.2337/diaspect.25.1.38

SEXUAL VITALITY AND DIET

A diet low in saturated fats and high in fibre enhances sexual vitality. It unclogs arteries, increasing free blood flow to all organs, including genitalia, resulting in more energy, less inflammation and more natural arousal.[75]

A healthy lifestyle and general overall health are directly related to sexual health. "...the impairment of sexual function may have a detrimental effect on self-esteem, body image, interpersonal relationships, and physical health in general, including fertility."[76]

Women experience a better mood when they eat dark chocolate, and it also has cognitive-enhancing qualities.[77][78][79]

Foods such as vanilla, black pepper, cacao, chili peppers, cloves, saffron, cinnamon, ginger, nutmeg and turmeric have mood-enhancing capabilities, which could assist in overall feelings of well-being.[80]

WEIGHT MANAGEMENT AND EXERCISE

By eating a healthy soup before a meal, the total calories consumed for the meal will be 20% lower.[81] An increase in fibre in your diet, can increase the success of weight management due to achieving that satisfied full feeling. There are far fewer calories in a plate full of vegetables vs. a plate full of steak and deep-fried potatoes.[82][83][84] Plant-based diets are low in saturated fat and high in fibre.

Vigorous exercise on a consistent basis is important for overall health. Bones are living tissue and need exercise to strengthen them. Heart and brain health are improved by consistent daily exercise by men and women of all ages.[85] The knowledge about the biological benefits of exercise is expanding every day.

Regular physical activity is crucial for women to protect against sexual dysfunction. Menopausal women have better body image with regular physical activity, improving self-esteem and emotional expression.[86]

[75] https://www.webmd.com/menopause/features/good-food-for-better-sex#1

[76] Tao P, Coates R, Maycock B. The impact of infertility on sexuality: A literature review. Australas Med J. 2011;4(11):620-627. doi:10.4066/AMJ.20111055

[77] https://www.thieme-connect.de/products/ejournals/html/10.1055/a-0588-5534#N69871

[78] Andrew Scholey, Lauren Owen, Effects of chocolate on cognitive function and mood: a systematic review, Nutrition Reviews, Volume 71, Issue 10, 1 October 2013, Pages 665–681, https://doi.org/10.1111/nure.12065

[79] Sumiyoshi E, Matsuzaki K, Sugimoto N, et al. Sub-Chronic Consumption of Dark Chocolate Enhances Cognitive Function and Releases Nerve Growth Factors: A Parallel-Group Randomized Trial. Nutrients. 2019;11(11):2800. Published 2019 Nov 16. doi:10.3390/nu11112800

[80] Smalheiser NR. A Neglected Link Between the Psychoactive Effects of Dietary Ingredients and Consciousness-Altering Drugs. Front Psychiatry. 2019;10:591. Published 2019 Aug 16. doi:10.3389/fpsyt.2019.00591/

[81] https://www.sciencedaily.com/releases/2007/05/070501142326.htm

[82] https://nutritionfacts.org/topics/fiber/

[83] Slavin JL. Dietary fiber and body weight. Nutrition. 2005 Mar;21(3):411-8. doi: 10.1016/j.nut.2004.08.018. PMID: 15797686.

[84] Howarth NC, Saltzman E, Roberts SB. Dietary fiber and weight regulation. Nutr Rev. 2001 May;59(5):129-39. doi: 10.1111/j.1753-4887.2001.tb07001.x. PMID: 11396693.

[85] Troy KL, Mancuso ME, Butler TA, Johnson JE. Exercise Early and Often: Effects of Physical Activity and Exercise on Women's Bone Health. Int J Environ Res Public Health. 2018 Apr 28;15(5):878. doi: 10.3390/ijerph15050878. PMID: 29710770; PMCID: PMC5981917.

[86] Mollaioli D, Ciocca G, Limoncin E, et al. Lifestyles and sexuality in men and women: the gender perspective in sexual medicine. Reprod Biol Endocrinol. 2020;18(1):10. Published 2020 Feb 17. doi:10.1186/s12958-019-0557-9

Index

Note: Italicised numbers are illustrations

Alexander I, Tsar of Russia 19
Africa (North) 155
Arnal, Armand 127
    La Chassagnette 125, 126, *126*, 127, *127*
    Michelin Star 127
artichokes 10, 44, 45, *45*, 47, 48, *49*, *50*, 51, 95, 188, *198–199*, 200, *221*, 223, 230
AT&T 65

Beck, Simone 159
Bertholle, Louisette 159
blood pressure 167, 179, 223, 224, 228, 230
Bocuse, Paul 88, 94, 95, 96, 97
Bonaparte, Napoleon 19
Brazier, Eugénie 8, 93, 94, 95, *95*, 98
books
    Brazier, Eugénie. *La Mère Brazier, Mother of Modern French Cooking*, Rizzoli, (2014). *95*
    Child, Julia; Beck, Simone; Bertholle, Louisette. *Mastering the Art of French Cooking*, Knopf, *(1961). 159*
    Dumas, Alexandre. *The Count of Monte Cristo*, Simon and Schuster, (1844). 154
    Jensen, Tara. *A Baker's Year: Twelve Months of Baking and Living the Simple Life at the Smoke Signals Bakery*, Macmillan Publishers (2018) *141*
    Mayle, Peter. *A Year in Provence*, Knopf, (1990). 118
    Mazzeo, Tilar J. *The Widow Clicquot: The Story of a Champagne Empire and the Woman Who Ruled It*, Harper, (2008). 18
    Owens, Sarah. *Sourdough: Recipes for Rustic Fermented Breads, Sweets, Savories and More*, Roost Books, (2015). 35
    Sroufe, Del. *The China Study Cookbook*, BenBella Books, (2004). 86-87, 206
breads
    Baguette (Classic) *162*, 163, *170*, 171–172, 200
    Classic Banana Bread 67, *84*, 85, 200
    Carob Apricot Sourdough Bread 34, *35*, *200*
    Dad and Stella's Cornbread with a Surprise *82*, *83*, 201
    Sweet Potato Walnut Bread (Classic French Country) 174, 175–176, *177*, 202
breakfast
    Cherry Clafoutis 146, *147*, 200
    Crêpes (Ancient) 106, *107*, 201

cakes
    Lemon Cake (Gâteau d'Arles) *4, 67, 138, 139*, 201
    Plum and Cherry Torte (Inspired by French Mirabelle Tart) 47, 56, *57*, 201
Canada 225
carbohydrates 225
carob 35, 98, 105, 180, 200, 218, 229
celiac 145
"Cheese"
    Cashew (Cultured) "Cheese" 32, *33*, 200
"Cheese" Sauce 9, 130, *131*, 132, 200, 202, 206
"Gruyère Cheese" *162*, 163, 202, 211
"Parmesan Cheese" 137, *162*, 163, 202, 212
cheesecakes
    Blackcurrant and Blueberry Cheesecake *128*, 129, *129*
    Chocolate Cheesecake with Yoghurt Ganache 180, *181*, 182, 200
    Lemon Lavender Luxury Cheesecake 67, 124, *124*, *144*, 145, 201
    Strawberry Rhubarb Champagne Cheesecake 24, *25*, 26, *27*, 201
    Vive la France Cheesecake 190, *190*, 192, 193, 202
Child, Julia 8, 77, 158, *158*, 159, 163, 201
    Child, Paul – (husband) 158, 159
    CIA (OSS) 159
    L'École des Trois Gourmandes, Paris 159
    The French Chef television program 159
    French Onion Soup 159, *162*, 163, 201, 211, 212
    Légion d'Honneur award *159*
    Jones, Judith (Knopf Publishing) 159
    Public Broadcasting System (PBS) 159
    Schlesinger Library, Radcliffe Institute, Harvard University 158
    shark repellent 159
cholesterol reduction 47, 146, 224
Connally, James (son) 189

dairy 52, 67, 85, 146, 192, 203, 212, 219, 224–227
diabetes 9, 65, 73, 225-226, 229, 231
Driscoll's 59
Dumas, Alexandre 154

Everett, Aaron (father) 40, *40*, 43
Everett, Mary (mother) 40, *40*, 43, 85, 159, 190
Everett, Tom (brother) 40, *40*, 43, *43*
Everett, Roy (paternal grandfather) 60, 63, *63*, *64*, 65, *73*
    army mess kit and canteen *60–61*, *63*
Everett, Stella (paternal grandmother) 8, 63, 64, *64*, 65, *65*, 66, 67, 71, 73, 77, 82, 201
    type 2 diabetes 65, 73

fat and saturated fats 223, 225–227, 230–231
fibre 225, 227, 228, 231
Flavour with Benefits
    breakfast 66
    function of liver 47
    health and weight 66
    "I'll Have What She's Having" *128*, 129, *129*
    importance of flavour 67
    oatmeal 67
    women's health 67
Flavour with Benefits: Sicily & Calabria 190, *194–197*
Food as medicine 8–10, 44, *45*, 222–224
    artichokes 10, 44, 45, *45*, 47, 48, *49*, *50*, 51, 95, 188, *198-199*, 200, *221*, 223, 230
    doctor prescribing artichokes 10, 44, 47
France
    Aix-en-Provence 122
    Arles 10, 29, 118, *118*, 119, *119*, 120–121, *120-121*, 122, 125, 138, 149, 201
    Roman Amphitheatre 118, 121, *121*
    Avignon 122
    Les Baux-de-Provence *116–117*
    La Belle France 188
    Biscuit Rose de Reims 24, *25*, 26, 28, *28*, 29, 200
    blue cheese 55, 82, *83*
    La Bresse 62, *62*, 63

Bollinger, Lily 15-16
Bonaparte, Napoleon 19
Bouzy 16, *16*, 17, *17*
Burgundy 8, 10, 61–71, *68-71*, *70*, 71, *71*, 73, 167
    wine and cheese 70, *70*
       château *70*
       Cistercian monks 71
       Côte d'Or 71
       Route des Grands Crus 71
       Côte de Beaune 71
       Côte de Nuits 71
       UNESCO World Heritage status 71
       vineyards *68-69*, *70*, 71, *71*
Calanques 10, *152–153*, 160, *160*
    Calanque d'En-Vau Beach 191, *191*
    Parc National des Calanques 160, *160*
Camargue 10, 122, 125, *125*
    horses of 125, *125*
Cassis 160, *160*, 161, *161*
    Château de Cassis 161, *161*
    Crème de Cassis 167, 179, 185, 200
    Falaises de Cassis 160, *161*
    wine 160
Cannes Film Festival 118
Chagall, Marc (artist) 42
Champagne houses
    Bernard Tornay Champagnes 17, *17*
    Champagne House of Moët & Chandon, Dom Pérignon 15
    Champagne Bollinger 15, 16
    Champagne Pommery 16
    Champagne Taittinger 15
    Louis Roederer 15
    Pol Roger Champagne House 20
    Veuve Clicquot (Company) 8, 15, 17, 18, *18*, 19, *19*, 20, *20*, 21, *21*, *22–23*
       Bold Woman Awards 20
       "bottle of the Widow" 19
       cellars of 17, 18, *19*, 20, 21
       headquarters Veuve Clicquot, Reims 22
       Pantone 137c (type of yellow) 20
Château des Baux-de-Provence 122, *122*, 123, *123*
Clicquot, Barbe-Nicole 8, 16–20, 190
Clicquot, François (husband of Barbe-Nicole) 19
Curnonsky, Prince 95
Épernay 15, *15*, 18, 23, *23*
flamingos 125
Fossier, Maison 24, 29
Le Havre 40
Hautvillers 16, *16*
Kruth 62, 63
Lorraine 10, 42, 47
Lyon 8, 10, 71, *88–91*, 92, *92*, 93, *93*, 94, 95, 96, *96*, 97, *97*, 98, 118
    La Basilique Notre-Dame de Fourvière *90*, *92*, 93, *93*
    Col de la Luère in Pollionnay (Restaurant on) 95
    Les Halles de Lyon Paul Bocuse *88–89*, *96*, 97, *97*
    Lyonnaise cuisine 94
    Les Mères de Lyon 92–95
    La Mère Brazier (restaurant) 93, 95, *95*
    Pont de la Feuillée (bridge over the River Saône) 96, *96*
    Tête d'Or (Park) 93, 94, *94*
    View of Lyon from La Basilique de Notre-Dame de Fourvière *90*, *92*, 93, *93*
    "The Weight of Oneself" statue 92, *92*

Marseille 8, 10, 92, 153, 154–155, *154–155*, *156–157*, 158, *158*, 159, 160, 186, *186*
    Aix-Marseille University 156, *156*
    Basilique Notre-Dame de la Garde 154, *155*
    bouillabaisse soup 155
    Château du Pharo 154
    Château Borély founded by Greeks 154
    Child, Julia 158, *158*, 159
    L'Épuisette (restaurant) 155
       Chef Guillaume Sourrieu 155
       Michelin star 155
       Sunset view *183*
    L'Île d'If 154
       The Count of Monte Cristo 154
    La Marseillaise 154
    Old Port (Vieux Port) 154, *154–157*
    Palais Longchamp 154
    Resistance in World War II 154
    Vallons des Auffes *156–157*
Mediterranean 10, 125, *152–153*, 154, 167, *186–187*
Les Mères de Lyon *92–95*
    la Mère Brazier *94*, 95, *95*
    la Mère Guy 94
    la Mère Fillioux 94
    la Mère Léa 94
Melz 8, 10, 40–48, *41-47*, 62
    artichoke 10, 44, 45, *45*, 47, 48, 49, 50, 51
    Cathédrale Saint-Étienne de Metz 41, *41*, 42, *42*, 46, *46*
    Chagall, Marc 42
    Gregorian chant 42
    doctor and artichoke 10, 44, 47
    École Maternelle, Fort Moselle 42, *42*, 43
    Marché Couvert de Metz (covered market) 44, *44*, 45, *45*, 47
    Moselle River *38–39*, 42
    Temple Neuf *38–39*
    Seille River 42
Nuits-Saint-Georges *68–69*, 71
Paris 10, 18, 92, 154, 159, 189
    L'École des Trois Gourmandes, Paris 159
    Pont Grenelle Statue of Liberty 189
    Seine River, 189
Provence 8, 10, 116–123, *116–123*, 124, 145, 154, 160, *160*
    Les Alpilles 122, *122*
    Château des Baux-de-Provence 122, *122*, 123, *123*
Reims 16, 18, 19, 20, *22–23*, 24
    Romans 20
    cellars/caves *19*, 20
    headquarters Veuve Clicquot, Reims 18, *18*, 19, *19*, 20, *20*, *21–23*
Rhône River 93, 118, 120, *120*, 123, 125, 127
riddling 19
Saône River 93, *93*, 96
Saint-Rémy-de-Provence 124
Seine River, 189
Stairway to Heaven 20, *20*
Ventron 61, 62
Les Veuves or Widows
    Bollinger, Madame Lily 15, 16
    Clicquot, Madame Barbe-Nicole 8, 16, 18, 19, 20, 190
    Henriot, Madame Apolline 16
    Laurent-Perrier, Madame Mathilde-Émilie 16
    Pommery, Madame Louise 16
    selling champagne to Royalty 16, 17
Vosges 8, 10, 62, *62*, 71

wine 16, 17, 19, *19, 20, 44, 70,* 71, 94, 102, 106, 118, 160, 163, 204
    Grand Cru 71
    Premier Cru 71
  Terroir 71
Fulbright Scholarship 40

genetic modification, European regulations 97
Great Depression 8, 65, 82

heart health 203, 216, 218, 226, 230

"I'll Have What She's Having" *128–129,* 129
Italy 8, 155, 190, 194, *194–195*
  Calabria *194–195,* 197
    Pentedattilo *194–195*
    Rogolino, Giovanna (maternal grandmother) 190, *197*
    Rogolino, Carlo (maternal grandfather) 190, *197*
    Rogolino, Antonino (uncle) *197*
  Sicily 190, *196, 197*
    Greek Temple of Segesta, Calatafimi 196, *196*
    Praetorian Fountain, Palermo 196, *196*
    swimming pool at house, Collesano 195, *195*
    Lasagna Verde with Asparagus 196, *196*
    Sicilian Kiwi Sorbet 197, *197*
ingredients alternatives
  Applesauce, unsweetened 86, 138, 202, 204
  "Beef" Broth 163, 202, 204
  Buttermilk Substitute 202, 205
  Date Purée 86, 202, 208
  Flax "eggs" 9, 59, 85, 106, 185, 202, 210
  "Gruyère Cheese" *162,* 163, 202, 211
  Hard Boiled "Eggs" (Faux Oeuf Dur) 164, *165, 202, 209*
  "Parmesan Cheese" *137, 162,* 163, 202, 212
  Sugar (Decorating) Revisited 146, 202, 208
  Sweet Potato Purée 86, 202, 213

Jensen, Tara 141

Karissa's Vegan Kitchen 214
King Arthur Baking Company 35, 172, 176

liver health 44, 47, 48, 51, 230
London Daily Mail (quote by Lily Bollinger) 15

maca 67, 98, 105, 180, 218, 229
mains – meat, fish and dairy
  Chicken (Roasted Spatchcock) and Vegetables *76,* 77–78, 200
  Coffee-Rub Ribeye Steak (Grilled) 130, *131,* 201
  Quiche Lorraine Nue (Naked Quiche Lorraine) 47, *54,* 55, 201
  Sea Bass Cassis *166,* 167, 201
Les Mères de Lyon 92–95
  la Mère Brazier 94, 95, *95*
  la Mère Guy 94
  la Mère Fillioux 94
  la Mère Léa 94
  la Mère Brigousse 98
Marckwald, Dorothy (interior decorator for SS United States) 40
Mayle, Peter 118
Mazzeo, Tilar J. 18, 19
Medieval cuisine 106
Michelin stars 93, 95, 127, 155

military – World War I
  American Expeditionary Force (AEF) (1917–1918) 63
  German forces (1917–1918) 63
military – World War II
  French Resistance 154
Miller, Mary, 134
Mistral winds 118
monk fruit (discussion) 9, 218, 223, 228
Monroe, Marilyn 20

Owens, Sarah 35

pastries
  Biscuit Rose de Reims (Tribute to) *28, 29,* 200
  Chocolate Donuts with Chocolate Frosting 86, *87,* 200
  Chocolate (Double) Fudge Brownies 67, *184,* 185, 200
  Chocolate Mousse – Avocado Surprise 67, *104,* 105, 201
  Tétons De Vénus Cakes 98, *99,* 100–*101, 202*
Picasso, Pablo 118
pies, tarts and fruit desserts
  Blueberry (Maple) Deep-Dish Pie – Tribute to Vincent Van Gogh:
    The Starry Night 124, *124,* 140–141, *142–143,* 200
  Pears (Festive Beaujolais Poached) 102, *103,* 201
  Raspberry Oatmeal Bars *58,* 59, 201
  Rhubarb Tart *148,* 149, *150,* 151, 201
plant-based meal 67, 73
protein 223, 225, 227

Queen Elizabeth 16
quotes
  Bocuse, Paul (about La Mère Brazier) 94
  Bollinger, Lily (about champagne) 15
  Child, Julia (about French cooking) 159
  Clicquot, Madame Barbe-Nicole (to her great-granddaughter) 18
  poultry supplier for Madame Eugénie Brazier 95
  Van Gogh, Vincent (about "yellow") 124

Rasmussen, Lori 151
recipes – A Toast to the Widows of Champagne
  Biscuit Rose de Reims – Tribute to *28, 29,* 201
  Carob Apricot Whole Wheat Sourdough Bread *34, 35–36, 200*
  Cashew (Cultured) "Cheese" *32, 33,* 201
  Crunchy Kale, Fennel & Cabbage Salad *30, 31,* 201
  Strawberry Rhubarb Champagne Cheesecake 24, *25, 26, 27,* 202
recipes – Metz and the Miracle of an Artichoke
  Artichoke Hummus 47, *50,* 51, 200
  Artichokes (Steamed) with Mustard Sauce 47, 48, *49,* 51, 200
  Asparagus (Steamed) with "Hollandaise" Sauce 52, *53,* 200
  Plum and Cherry Torte (Inspired by French Mirabelle Tart) 47,
    56, *57,* 201
  Quiche Lorraine Nue (Naked Quiche Lorraine) 47, *54,* 55, 201
  Raspberry Oatmeal Bars *58,* 59, 201
recipes – Courage, Sacrifice and Love: Vosges and Burgundy
  Chicken (Roasted Spatchcock) and Vegetables *76,* 77–78, 200
  Chocolate Donuts with Chocolate Frosting 86, *87,* 200
  Classic Banana Bread 67, *84,* 85, 200
  Crudités with Dipping Sauce 67, *72,* 73, 201
  Dad and Stella's Cornbread with a Surprise 82, *83,* 201
  Leek, Potato, Onion & Edamame Soup 74, *75,* 201
  Sweet Potato Fries 67, *80,* 81, 201
recipes – Lyon: The Capital of French Cuisine
  Cauliflower Steak on Cauliflower Potato Soup 110, *111,* 200
  Chocolate Mousse – Avocado Surprise 67, *104,* 105, 201

Crêpes (Ancient) 106, *107*, 201
Pear, Raspberry & Quinoa Salad with Aged Balsamic Vinegar *108*, 109, 201
Pears (Festive Beaujolais Poached) 102, *103*, 201
Potato Salad (French) *112*, 113, 164, *165*, *201*
Sweet Potatoes (Fancy Piped) *114, 115*, 201
Tétons De Vénus Cakes 98, *99*, 100–101, 202
recipes – Meandering through Provence
Asparagus (Steamed) with "Cheese" Sauce 130, *131*, 132, 200
Blueberry (Maple) Deep-Dish Pie – Tribute to Vincent Van Gogh: *The Starry Night* 124, *124*, 140–141, *142–143*, 200
Cherry Clafoutis 146, *147*, 200
Coffee-Rub Ribeye Steak (Grilled) 130, *131*, 201
Lavender Blueberry Dressing for a Summer Salad 134, *135*, 201
Lemon Cake (Gâteau d'Arles) *4, 67, 138, 139*, 201
Lemon Lavender Luxury Cheesecake 67, *124, 144*, 145, 201
Potatoes au Gratin (Gratin Dauphinois) *136*, 137, 201
Rhubarb Tart 148, 149, *150*, 151, 201
Zoodles (Sautéed) with Sweet Pepper Purée 130, *131*, 133, 202
recipes – Marseille: Mirror on the Mediterranean
Baguette (Classic) *162*, 163, *170*, 171–172, 200
Chocolate (Double) Fudge Brownies 67, *184*, 185, 200
Chocolate Cheesecake with Yoghurt Ganache 180, *181*, 182, 200
Chocolate Hummus Kissed by Crème de Cassis *178*, 179, 200
French Onion Soup – A Classic Revisited 159, *162*, 163, 201, 212
Frites Au Four (Baked French Fries) 67, 168, 169, 201
Salad Niçoise – Inspired by Julia Child 113, 164, *165*, 201
Sea Bass Cassis *166*, 167, 201
Sweet Potato Walnut Bread (Classic French Country) 174, 175–176, *177*, 202
recipe – It's Time to Leave
Vive la France Cheesecake 190, *190*, 192, 193
recipes – Alternative Ingredients
Applesauce, unsweetened 86, 138, 202, 204
"Beef" Broth 163, 202, 204
Buttermilk Substitute 202, 205
"Cheese" Sauce 130, *131*, 132, 200, 202, 206
Date Purée 86, 202, 208
Flax "eggs" 9, 59, 85, 106, 185, 202, 210
"Gruyère Cheese" *162*, 163, 202, 211
Hard Boiled "Eggs" (Faux Oeuf Dur) 164, *165*, 202, 209
"Parmesan Cheese" 137, *162*, 163, 202, 212
Sugar (Decorating) Revisited 146, 202, 208
Sweet Potato Purée 86, 202, 213
"Worcestershire" Sauce 163, 168, 202, 204, 214
Resources and tools 198
Rogolino, Giovanna maternal grandmother) 190, 197, *197*
Rogolino, Carlo (maternal grandfather) 190, 197, *197*
Rogolino, Antonino (uncle) 197, *197*
Royal Court (of Russia), in St Petersburg *19*

salads, sauces and dressings
Crunchy Kale, Fennel & Cabbage Salad *30, 31*, 201
Lavender Blueberry Dressing for a Summer Salad 134, *135*, 201
Pear, Raspberry & Quinoa Salad with Aged Balsamic Vinegar *108*, 109, 201
Salad Niçoise – Inspired by Julia Child 113, 164, *165*, 201
"Worcestershire" Sauce 163, 168, 202, 204, 214
sexual vitality 9, 67, 98, 190, 200–202, *203*, 218, 229, 231
side dishes
Artichokes (Steamed) with Mustard Sauce 47, 48, *49*, 51, 200
Asparagus (Steamed) with "Cheese" Sauce 130, *131*, 132, 200
Asparagus (Steamed) with "Hollandaise" Sauce 52, *53*, 200
Frites Au Four (Baked French Fries) 67, 168, 169, 201

Potato Salad (French) *112*, 113, 164, *165*, *201*
Potatoes au Gratin (Gratin Dauphinois) *136*, 137, 201
Sweet Potato Fries 67, *80*, 81, 201
Sweet Potatoes (Fancy Piped) 114, *115*, 201
Zoodles (Sautéed) with Sweet Pepper Purée 130, *131*, 133, 202
Small Changes, Big Benefits: A Nutrition Interlude 66–67
food changes 66–67
importance of flavour 66–67
snacks
Artichoke Hummus 47, *50*, 51, 200
Chocolate Hummus Kissed by Crème de Cassis *178*, 179, 200
Crudités with Dipping Sauce 67, *72*, 73, 201
soups
Leek, Potato, Onion & Edamame Soup 74, *75*, 201
Cauliflower Steak on Cauliflower Potato Soup 110, *111*, 200
French Onion Soup – A Classic Revisited 159, *162*, 163, 201, 212
SS United States 40, *40*
Stairway to Heaven 20, *20*

T. Colin Campbell Center for Nutrition Studies 86, 206, 208

United States 188
Connecticut 40, 43
Kansas 63, 64, 65
Little Rock, Arkansas 189
Arkansas Arts Center 189
Missouri 63
New York (City), NY 40, 189, 190
Ellis Island 190
Liberty Island, Bedloe Island 189
Statue of Liberty (Liberty Enlightening the World), Libertas 189, *189, 190*
Bartholdi, Frédéric Auguste, sculptor 189
de Laboulaye, Édouard René, abolitionist 189
Lazarus, Emma, poet, "The New Colossus" 189
Urquhart, Anne, interior decorator for SS United States *40*

Van Gogh, Vincent 118, 124, 200
quote 124
The Starry Night 124, 140, *142–143*
Viannay, Mathieu (La Mère Brazier) 95
Michelin rating *93*
vitamins and minerals 226

weight management 224, 228, 230-231
"The Weight of Oneself" 92, *92*
WikiHow 221
Winston Churchill 20
women of Champagne – The Widows
Bollinger, Lily 15, 16
Quote from 1961 London *Daily Mail* 15
Henriot, Apolline 16
Laurent-Perrier, Mathilde-Émilie 16
Pommery, Louise 16
Ponsardin, Madame (Veuve Clicquot) 16

Yellow (colour) 118, 124
Quote by Vincent Van Gogh 124

Selected Bibliography

Brazier, Eugénie. *La Mère Brazier: Mother of Modern French Cooking*, Rizzoli, 2014

Child, Julia; Beck, Simone; Bertholle, Louisette. *Mastering the Art of French Cooking*, Knopf, 1961

Dumas, Alexandre. *The Count of Monte Cristo*, Simon and Schuster, 1844

Jensen, Tara. *A Baker's Year: Twelve Months of Baking and Living the Simple Life at the Smoke Signals Bakery*, Macmillan Publishers, 2018

Mayle, Peter. *A Year in Provence*, Knopf, 1990

Mazzeo, Tilar J. *The Widow Clicquot: The Story of a Champagne Empire and the Woman Who Ruled It*, Harper, 2008

Owens, Sarah. *Sourdough: Recipes for Rustic Fermented Breads, Sweets, Savories, and More*, Roost Books, 2015

Sroufe, Del. *The China Study Cookbook*, BenBella Books, 2004

Acknowledgements

Who helped to put the "flavour" and the "benefits" into this journey? In writing this book, we have worked with, and been inspired by so many wonderful people and organizations.

Where would we be without the skills and dedication of Kerry West (thuddesign.com)? We have worked with Kerry for well over a decade on marketing collateral design and layout, website development and more. She has been an important contributor to the beauty and layout of this book. She has had to put up with our course changes on the development of the book and the downstream effects on having to do countless edits to the interior of the book. Kerry, thank you! The beautiful illustrations for the cover and the interior map were done by Camilla Charnock. Thank you for continuing to make edits for us. Your work is outstanding.

An important theme of the book is improving the nutritional quality of our meals without sacrificing flavour. The value of improved nutrition and a better understanding of the impacts on human health were inspired by Cathy's remote learning course with David Levitsky, PhD, Professor of Nutrition and Psychology at Cornell University, with the *Nutrition and Healthy Living* course and the additional course work with T. Colin Campbell, PhD's NutritionStudies.org, *Plant-Based Nutrition Program* also via eCornell. With this foundation of nutritional enlightenment, further inspiration was provided by the work of Drs. Thomas Campbell, Dean Cornish, Caldwell Esselstyn, Michael Greger, and Scott Stoll. A special thanks for Doug Lisle, PhD for his lectures and humour and to Rip Esselstyn, founder of Plant-Strong. Their work informs many of the recipes created in this book as we strive to bring healthy plant-based nutrition options to your plate.

Several people have been helpful in improving our knowledge of creating, publishing and marketing a book. These people include Judith Briles (The Book Shepherd) who has provided sage advice on our book journey, Amy Collins, Kelly Johnson and Joel Friedlander.

Editing is tough on authors. In our case we suspect it was harder on the editors. The book's message, format and authors posed the "herding cats" challenge. Garret McGrath gave us the first-cut on what was working and what wasn't. He took our hand drawn map and encouraged the use of original illustrations to make the book more unique and entertaining. Thanks Garret, you were right! Gabriella Sterio picked up the editing torch and capably guided us through the paces.

Daniel Milligan and Alexander Best provided much needed initial proofing, and Alexander suggested a couple of strategic edits that were brilliant and polished the spirit of the book. Alexander, you kept it short and sweet!

Using the Upwork platform we put together an international team of beta readers who provided feedback on the book through an initial impression reading and then a more detailed review process. That exercise helped us improve the quality of the reader's experience. We hope to build on elements of their suggestions in the next book, *Flavour with Benefits: Sicily & Calabria*. Thanks to the team including: Marina Zubakhina, Tracey Harbaugh, Sally Foster (near Bordeaux, France), Rachel O'Shea (www.therachelcate.com), Melissa Prideaux, Maria A. Van Norman (www.thisis40life.com), Natalie Bachiri (Blog: makeitfromscratchmom), Lisa Howard, Lee Ann Millar, Kathleen Ladelpha, Ivana Atanasova (Blog: Diary of Difference), Heidi Salter (Blog: yourtalentjourney.net), Gianna Marciarille, Emilie Nicole, Cath Lauria and Nancy Laverty-Snider, Rebecca Martin (Twitter @TheBeckyEdit).

We have valued the artistic expertise of Rebecca Finkel for interior book design consultation, and front and back cover design. Judith Briles and Casey Demchak provided insight and polish to the back cover copy.

Moving from the print version to an eBook format can seem a bit daunting. It isn't easy to keep the visual charm of a printed book full of panorama photos, food close-ups, vibrant colours and then convert it to an electronic platform. Zvonimir Bulaja, and Ward Salud, gave us the options we needed in a professional and timely manner. Thank you, gentlemen.

Thanks to Joan Stewart, Publicity Hound, for her sage advice and for recommending Wasabi Publicity and Michelle Tennant Nicholson's PR expertise.

Cathy would also like to thank her Instagram friends around the world for encouragement and support. Charley and Cathy both use Nikon® cameras including a D3300 and a Coolpix® 900 with assorted lenses. The visual joy and flavour captured in many of the images in this book is a lesson in perseverance, planning, good equipment and luck. Charley also uses a DJI Mavic® Air ("Thorlito") drone to provide an elevated perspective when rules and weather permit.

Authors' Bios

Cathy Connally's culinary career had an inauspicious start at nine years old, with the renovation of her mother's kitchen involving the Yellow Springs, Ohio fire department. Later, to the horror of a high school teacher in St. Peter, Minnesota, she would win a Betty Crocker Award, only because she was good at math. This vote of confidence would propel her into the field of internal audit in the global mining sector and eventually to a career as an entrepreneur in technology. A low-quality diet was causing health issues. Eating countless takeout meals while driving hours to put out project "fires", was leading to a slow train wreck on the health front. She recalled a lesson she had learned at five years old about food as medicine. This led to the birth of Flavour with Benefits, the pursuit of flavour that doesn't compromise on health. Cathy also loves adding a side dish of travel to her life, which has allowed her to visit over 60 countries. Relaxation involves cooking, baking and hiking.

To contact Cathy: *Instagram: @flavourwithbenefits*
Facebook: flavourwithbenefits Website: www.flavourwithbenefits.com

Charley Best decided after decades lounging as an entrepreneur, he would use his weekends and meditation time and add author to his list of hobbies. Overestimating his writing capabilities, this is his first completed project in years. His co-author, Cathy Connally, has given him a lot to chew on and now he is not only a believer in the positive effects of the Flavour with Benefits approach to nutrition and the enjoyment of delicious food, but he's also developed a stand-up comedy routine about the benefits. He loves hummingbirds and spends many hopeful hours by a window with a camera, willing the snow to melt and pining for the birds to return. He prefers the dainty photogenic female birds. The male birds are narcissistic, camera-shy, nectar-hogs, but admittedly their courtship acrobatics are spectacular.

To contact Charley: *Instagram @authorofyourowndestiny & Facebook: authorofyourowndestiny Twitter: @CharleyBest6*

Collesano Publishing
1000-121 Richmond St West
Toronto, ON M5H2K1
Canada

Library and Archives Canada registration (Legal Deposit) is available upon request.

Printed in Canada
Printed by Friesens Corporation
First Edition

ISBN: 978-1-7772649-2-5 (Hardcover)
ISBN: 978-1-7772649-1-8 (Kindle)

Book design: Kerry West, Thud Design, info@thuddesign.com
Book cover illustration and interior map illustration on page 11: Camilla Charnock (www.camillacharnock.com)
Cover design: Rebecca Finkel, F+P Graphic Design